After-School Prevention Programs
for At-Risk Students

Elaine Clanton Harpine

After-School Prevention Programs for At-Risk Students

Promoting Engagement and Academic Success

 Springer

Elaine Clanton Harpine
University of South Carolina Aiken
Aiken, SC, USA

ISBN 978-1-4614-7415-9   ISBN 978-1-4614-7416-6 (eBook)
DOI 10.1007/978-1-4614-7416-6
Springer New York Heidelberg Dordrecht London

Library of Congress Control Number: 2013939033

Printed on acid-free paper

Springer is part of Springer Science+Business Media (www.springer.com)

To my loving husband, Bill, for his
never-ending support and encouragement.

Preface

Ten years old, he was still classified as a first grader. Labeled "mildly mentally retarded" by the school psychologist, he received special instruction and tutoring through an Individualized Educational Program (IEP). He also attended an after-school program and worked with a mentor. All the same, he still could not read (not even at the pre-primer level), did not know any vowel or consonant sounds, and, furthermore, had absolutely no desire to learn to read. His mother had told him that he would never be able to read, and he had accepted this to be true. Therefore, he refused to even try. Two years after he was placed in a group-centered after-school intensive reading program, he's reading. His progress was slow, but he was now learning to read. Why? What made the difference?

Group-centered programs enable students to learn concepts that they have been unable to learn in the regular classroom or even through tutoring or traditional after-school programs. The key to group-centered programming is to combine learning and counseling into a single group program. Merely placing children in a group setting is not sufficient. It is the group-centered structure which makes this approach work.

This book is for those who work with students in an after-school program, particularly those who develop, plan, and select the curriculum and activities for after-school programs. The book incorporates step-by-step instructions to teach readers how to develop a year-long curriculum. Developing a year-long program is much different than developing a 1-hour or week-long session. By the end of this book, the reader will be able to create an effective year-long after-school group-centered prevention program.

This is the third book in a series about group-centered prevention. The first volume, *Group Interventions in Schools: Promoting Mental Health for At-Risk Children and Youth* (2008), introduced the concept of group-centered prevention and presented step-by-step directions for developing 1-hour pull-out style school-based interventions. The second book, *Group-Centered Prevention Programs for At-Risk Students* (2011), covered how to design intensive 10-hour week-long motivational group-centered prevention programs. This third book gives step-by-step directions for developing year-long after-school programs. The three books may be used together or independently. They can be used for workshops, continuing education courses, in-service training, parent groups, or counselors who wish to add to their knowledge in group prevention. Each book could easily be included in an under-graduate or graduate class discussing group prevention, school-based interventions, community after-school programs, at-risk children and teens, or issues in educa-tional psychology.

This book explains the theoretical reasons for using an interactive group-centered approach in after-school programs. This book also identifies the unique needs of an ongoing year-long after-school program as opposed to a short-term program. All too often, after-school workers try to use curriculum or programming ideas intended for short-term pull-out interventions. Children engaged in 1-week programs have totally different needs than children participating in a year-long program. This book identifies and tells how to fulfill these year-long programming needs.

Each chapter begins with a brief case study. Chapter 1 discusses selecting par-ticipants, organizing for different ages, and setting up and developing an after-school program. Multicultural and gender considerations are discussed. Chapter 2 examines hands-on learning techniques in a group-centered after-school program, emphasizing the theories that support group-centered prevention. Chapter 3 talks about incorporating counseling techniques and mental wellness into the design for an effective after-school program. Step-by-step examples for writing learning cen-ter workstations highlight both counseling and learning issues. Chapter 4 will cover how to use intrinsic motivation and hands-on skill-building interventions to bring about desired behavioral change and academic learning. Learning to use motivation constructively is essential in after-school programs. Chapter 5 shows how group process brings about change, stressing the importance of cohesion. It includes inter-ventions to develop cohesion during an after-school program and looks at creative group-centered therapy techniques. Chapter 6 provides ready-to-use methods to maintain positive, effective group interaction during a year-long program. Guidelines for appropriate self-disclosure, group behavior, and initiating positive feedback are discussed. Chapter 7 will discuss how to handle conflicts with both children and adolescents. There are conflicts and problems in every group. Chapter 8 discusses how after-school programs fit into the overall learning environment. Observational exercises and group-centered interventions will help those using the book to apply what they have learned back to the after-school setting.

Each chapter ends with a ready-to-use group-centered intervention that can be used at a learning center workstation. Each learning center example represents a specific theoretical concept and demonstrates how to use that concept in a year-long after-school program. A special table of contents lists all of the interventions. This makes it simple to select a learning center example or refer to an example as you follow each step in the design process.

Each chapter is also packed with group-focused observational activities and troubleshooting checklists specifically geared to after-school programs. A case study example of a group-centered after-school prevention program, the *Reading Orienteering Club,* is used throughout the book to illustrate how to organize and facilitate a year-long program but a year-long program packet is much too lengthy to be included in its entirety in an appendix. The *Reading Orienteering Club* is listed in the reference section for those who are interested in learning more about the program.

The 10-year-old student from the opening example participates in the *Reading Orienteering Club*, a year-long group-centered after-school community-based prevention program that emphasizes phonological awareness, reading and writing, spelling, and intensive hands-on instruction. It incorporates group counseling interventions teaching the children to manage anger, interact and work with others in a group, handle stress and anxiety, develop social skills, counter bullying, and work through feelings of failure.

A case study example of a typical session is included. The case example is from the *Reading Orienteering Club*, a group-centered after-school prevention program.

Case Example

The session begins with an action story that emphasizes the vowel sound for the day. A story talks about how *Andy the Ant* and *Gail the Snail* learn to share, take turns, and become better friends. The children help tell the story by acting out portions of the story. The short A sound, which the children learned about during the previous session, is reviewed. A fun vowel-clustered action story helps children review and begin to practice vowel sounds.

The children then go out to the hands-on learning center workstations. The rooms are laid out by points on a compass—North, Northeast, Northwest, and so on. Eight different learning center workstations correspond to the points on the compass. Each compass workstation has a notebook with a different assignment for the day. Children travel around the room to all eight workstations but may start at any workstation. Today, the children work on the seven different vowel combinations that use the long A vowel sound: AI, AY, EI, EY, EA, EIGH, and silent E.

At the North station, the children read a story about *Gail the Snail*. The story emphasizes the seven vowel combinations that can be used to make the long A vowel sound. The story ends with a challenge step. Children are invited to *Take the Challenge* and write their own imaginative ending to the story. This helps children practice reading and writing the day's vowel sound. The story ending asks the child to decide how to solve a problem (counseling skill) that *Gail the Snail* is having in her group.

At the Northeast workstation, children are trying to *capture* as many *tricky words* as possible. The words emphasize the long A sound being studied today. To capture a word means to find a word that the child cannot read or spell—a word that the child does not know. The children will then use the *4-step method* (say the word, spell the word with letters, write the word, and give a definition and sentence using the word). The children are looking for tricky words by reading a long paper *grapevine* which stretches halfway across the room. Each child is trying to find five tricky words.

Everyone is trying to capture as many words as possible today and will add their tricky words to their word list as they travel around to each station. The word list is being used for today's craft project, but the craft project is like a puzzle. The children have to figure out what they are making by the clues at each workstation. A captured word is a word that the child does not know or cannot read or spell; therefore, children are practicing and learning new words as they travel around the room to each station. The children learn to work together as they move from station to station with different group members. The day's group counseling concept is taking turns while sharing.

The Northwest station features more than ten books graded by ability and labeled as Step 1....Step 3. The children start at Step 1, select one book, and read to the station helper(s) until they capture five new tricky words to add to their word list. Children who are struggling may find all five tricky words at Step 1. Other children may continue selecting books and reading until they get to Step 3. Naturally, the books are graded by ability; therefore, no one is given a book that they cannot read and there are always challenge books to encourage even the most reluctant of readers. Motivation and self-efficacy are key group skills being practiced at this workstation. Again, the children capture tricky words and add these words to their word list using the *4-step method*.

The East workstation stresses healthy eating, sometimes with a healthy snack. Today, the children are sorting pictures of healthy and not-so-healthy foods into baskets. The words *cake* and *steak* emphasize two of the not-so-healthy food choices and also emphasize the vowel sound being studied today. Children search through the pictures to find five foods that use the long A vowel sound. They practice spelling the words out loud and then add the words to their word lists.

When the children go South, they use letter tiles to spell words as the helper reads a designated list of words. Each time they capture a word, they stop and write the word down on their word list, look up a definition in the dictionary, and think of a sentence using the word. The idea is not just to capture words but to learn them. Students must take turns and share the letter tiles. They also learn to help each other use the dictionary. Working together as a team (without competition) is stressed.

At the Southeast station, before the children start, they are told that they must make a paper plate face puppet. They read simple step-by-step instructions to make a paper plate puppet. Each child is given a paper plate on which to draw a face. They add a handle to their paper plate face to make it into a puppet. They use their word strips to make hair. The guys always seem to want to cut their strips and make spikey hair out of the word strips; girls frequently like to make long curls or ringlets. Creativity is always encouraged. The only rule is that you must be able to read all of the captured words. Remember, these are words that the children did not know at the beginning of the session. If they are still having trouble with any of the words, the station helper helps the child follow the *4-steps*.

At the Southwest station, each child practices reading a puppet play. The play is written with both easy and challenging puppet parts so that everyone will be able to participate.

When they go West, the children select a chapter book. This station is repeated for 6 weeks. They will spend 6 weeks reading the book they select. By the end of the 6 weeks, the children will design and make a costume for the main character and give a report about the book for a videotaped pretend TV show. Reading for details to design a costume helps children focus attention and look for details in a story. Once again, the children use the *step system,* starting at Step 1 to select a book at their reading level. There are over 30 books laid out at the three steps. The idea is to rebuild self-efficacy (belief that they can succeed) by encouraging the children to read harder and harder books. Using steps instead of reading levels or grades saves children from being embarrassed. It also encourages children who might settle for simply reading the easiest book available to search for harder books in order to find the five tricky words that they need for their puppet. If they do not capture five words at Step 1, they go on to Step 2 or Step 3. Also, they follow step-by-step instructions and make colorful bookmarks so that they will be able to find their place in the chapter book each session. Following step-by-step instructions helps to increase comprehension because you cannot make a project if you do not understand the words you have read.

It should be mentioned that children do not move around the compass points in groups or move between workstations at designated intervals. Everyone works at their own pace, spending more time where they are struggling. This helps to individualize instruction since there are helpers at each workstation to help anyone who is having difficulty with the task. In one 2-hour session, the children have practiced reading, writing, spelling, focusing their attention, comprehension, following step-by-step instructions, learning new words, and practicing a specific vowel cluster for the day. They have also practiced interaction and group skills, focusing attention on a specific task, social skills and working nicely with others in a group, leadership and team building without competition, and rebuilding self-efficacy.

Intensive reading instruction in a group-centered atmosphere is the goal. This is a perfect approach for an after-school program because it can accommodate a variety of ages and allow each child to work at their own ability level. The group-centered approach also incorporates the healing therapeutic power of group process by encouraging the children to work together in a cohesive group atmosphere. The puppet play and the pretend TV show give the children opportunities to practice leadership and group process skills.

Easy Reference Guide to Group-Centered Learning Center Interventions

This easy reference guide will make it easier for those wishing to find an example of a particular type of learning center at a glance. All of the interventions in this book are written as learning center examples. I have used reading as the academic focus for the learning centers in order to show continuity.

Acknowledgments

I wish to express my appreciation to Judy Jones, my editor and friend, for her support and help in the development of this book series on group-centered prevention programs. I also want to thank my husband, Bill, for his love and support throughout the entire project and for his patience and helpful comments on the text. I would like to thank my three children, David, Virginia, and Christina, who have all worked as reading tutors in my reading programs. A very special thank you goes to Harry Sampson, Rev. Dr. George Howle, the United Methodist Women of St. John's United Methodist Church in Aiken, South Carolina, and all of the members and workers from St. John's who believed in this program and who financially sponsored and supported our community-wide after-school prevention project. Thank you to Jacqui DeMinck, Ashley Padgett, and Laura Paxton for their loyal work and support each week. A special thank you also goes to all of the children, youth, university students, community volunteers, parents, teachers, and university faculty whom I have had the pleasure of working with while developing group-centered after-school prevention programs.

Contents

Chapter 1
Organizing an After-School Program

The director of a local community-based after-school program cheerfully explained that her organization had just received a grant to expand their after-school program to include a prevention project with children who were failing in school. Someone asked what type of program she would be offering, and she explained, "We're mostly going to focus on homework help and field trips. We bought an evidence-based program, but it looks like so much work. We may use a few pieces of it; but by the time the children get off the bus, eat a snack, and do their homework, there's just not time to do all that stuff. Besides, the children love going on field trips."

Approximately eight million students in the United States attend after-school programs (Durlak et al. 2010a). After-school programs range from homework assistance to organized recreational games, and to academically oriented skills training and prevention activities. The US government spends about $1 billion annually to support after-school programs (US Department of Education 2009). This expense is justifiable if it helps students improve in school. Indeed, one estimate suggests that approximately $1.4 billion could be saved each year from the criminal justice system if a mere 1 % of those male students who drop out before graduation were to finish high school (Levin and Holmes 2005). Failure in school leads to failure in life (Miech et al. 2005).

Academic failure stands as a major cause of adolescent aggression, bullying, and violence (Greene and Winters 2006). If after-school programs can help reduce academic failure and reduce the number of students dropping out before graduation, then after-school programs would be a major asset in education. Unfortunately, research shows that after-school programs consisting primarily of homework help and recreational activities neither improve student grades nor reduce the high school dropout rate (Sheldon et al. 2010; Shernoff 2010). Presenting a wide variety of after-school activities and offering staff training have also not reduced academic failure (Pierce et al. 2010). What we need is a way to make after-school programs more effective.

E. Clanton Harpine, *After-School Prevention Programs for At-Risk Students: Promoting Engagement and Academic Success*, DOI 10.1007/978-1-4614-7416-6_1, © Springer Science+Business Media New York 2013

After-School Programs Must Change

In the June 2010 special issue of the *American Journal of Community Psychology*, researchers stated that there is a need to change how we conduct after-school programs (Durlak et al. 2010b; Smith et al. 2010; Yohalem and Wilson-Ahlstrom 2010). That change includes not only the types of after-school programs (homework and recreation) but also the ways that we organize and direct them. Researchers establish that if we really want to improve after-school programming, we must move beyond after-school programs that serve as child care facilities and recreation centers. We must move beyond programs that measure success merely through attendance figures (Hirsch et al. 2010). After-school programs began as safe havens for children of working parents, but merely providing a safe place for children to gather after school cannot be enough (Durlak et al. 2010a). Today, we need after-school programs that do more than merely warehouse children and teens after school. We need programs that also measure success in terms of actual academic improvement as well as healthy mental and psychological development and well-being. Such changes will not be easy to accomplish unless attitudes about after-school programming change. This book can help those who work with after-school programs to bring about these changes.

A student who attended a community-based after-school program for 4 years without any sign of improvement exemplifies the need for change. The after-school program offered an individual mentor for homework help. Once homework was complete, the mentor and child often played a game together. Unfortunately during the 4 years, this child fell further and further behind in school despite the child's faithful attendance at the program. The child was retained twice in school, started fighting with classmates, and could neither read at grade level nor work math problems at grade level. After one horrendous fight, the child was sent to the county's alternative school for behavioral problems. After several months, there was still no improvement. Eventually, the child was enrolled in my *Reading Orienteering Club* (Clanton Harpine 2013a, b), an intensive group-centered after-school prevention program for reading problems. Two years later, the child reads at grade level, improving daily in comprehension, and displays dramatically better behavior in school. This type of after-school program, the *Reading Orienteering Club*, does not offer homework help or recreation; instead, it retrains children by teaching a new approach to reading. It is a group-centered after-school prevention program focused on academic change in order to prevent academic failure and help bring about mental and psychological wellness.

In this book, we will learn how to design such a group-centered after-school prevention program. The focus of your after-school program need not be reading, as mine is, but your program needs to include an academic component to prevent academic failure and foster mental wellness. Your program could instead feature math, science, history, or literature. I work with at-risk students who are failing; therefore, reading is where I begin. The examples that I present in this book also discuss reading, not because I am trying to convince you to develop a reading program, but because I want to demonstrate the thought process that I have gone through in developing a successful year-long group-centered after-school program.

Selecting a Group Approach for Your After-School Program

There are many different types of group programs. If you are setting up a new after-school program or redesigning your existing after-school program, you must be careful when you select a curriculum or a group approach. Let's look at some of the advantages of the group-centered approach over other techniques being offered.

Evidence-based programs. Programs which produce change documented by randomized controlled studies are often defined as evidence-based programs (Kazdin 2008). To improve after-school programs, many funding agencies, schools, and community organizations insist upon using only evidence-based programs. An evidence-based program is an excellent idea, but we must understand that simply purchasing an evidence-based program will not guarantee that students improve. There is no way to insure that the after-school program will use the evidence-based program as it was written. It is not enough to say that I have purchased an evidence-based program. If that evidence-based program is not being used as designed, then the evidence which supports the program is irrelevant (McHugh and Barlow 2010). Selecting bits and pieces of a program or changing a program can destroy the evidence-based value of the purchased program (Riggs et al. 2010). Any changes that you make to an evidence-based program will alter its effectiveness. Poor implementation (how the program was conducted) can also prevent an evidence-based program from working successfully and thereby nullify any advantages that an evidence-based program might offer (Langley et al. 2010). Regardless of how well designed a program may be, the success of the evidence-based program will be less than intended if it is poorly implemented; therefore, implementation is an important component for measuring the effectiveness of any after-school program (Durlak and Dupre 2008). Evidence-based programs must be implemented properly or they will not work. Recent research found that even when groups used the same evidence-based program, received the same training, and had supervision overseeing their use of the program, groups in a controlled study did not necessarily receive the same results from the same program (Laska et al. 2013). Therefore, while the idea of using evidence-based programs is to be applauded, the implementation or the manner in which those evidence-based programs are presently being implemented is making the use of evidence-based programs less than successful. We need a way to make sure that evidence-based programs give the same results in a community-based after-school program as demonstrated in a randomized controlled study.

Training manuals. Some researchers call for stronger reliance on training and program manuals to improve implementation (Kulic et al. 2004), but training programs and manuals are not always effective (Kazak et al. 2010). The existence of a manual, no matter how well written, does not guarantee that the person implementing the program will follow the directions in the manual (Nation et al. 2003).

Technology. There is also a trend toward providing the latest in technological hardware. While iPads and SMART Boards can add a new dimension to education and have their place, computers cannot teach a child who is totally confused or motivate a child who has given up and refuses to try. Computers can offer wonderful research options, historical presentations, and opportunities to practice and correct mistakes, but computers cannot provide the therapeutic benefits of group process, social skills, or the feeling of belonging that comes from working in a cohesive group. Yes, computers can be an asset, but if you plan your entire program on computers, your program will fail.

Prevention programs. We hear a lot about prevention programs these days, especially since after-school prevention programs are demonstrating some measure of success. Children can and do improve, both academically and in overall wellness, through prevention programs (Prilleltensky et al. 2001; Brooks-Gunn 2003; Greenberg et al. 2001). Again, the type of prevention program and how the program is conducted determine whether the prevention program is successful or not. We need to be careful, however. Just because an after-school program carries the prevention label does not mean that the program will necessarily be effective. Too many programs use the prevention label but do not follow the principles of group prevention. Prevention groups always stress group process, group interaction, and positive group cohesion (Conyne and Clanton Harpine 2010).

Looking at the Complete Program

Robert Granger (2010) from the William T. Grant Foundation suggests that we must begin to look at the "in-program processes" if we are to actually improve program quality in after-school programming. Simply buying an evidence-based program, using a training manual, adopting the latest computer gadget, or attaching a prevention label is not enough to actually bring about change in after-school programming (Granger et al. 2007). Examining the "in-program processes" would require that we look at group techniques, teaching strategies, motivators, communication strategies, and implementation (how the program was conducted) not only in our evaluation procedures but in our design of effective after-school programs as well (Granger 2010).

It will be our goal in this book to show how to design a group-centered after-school prevention program. We will not look for quick fixes. We will look at the "in-program processes" and develop a new approach to after-school programming.

Redesigning After-School Programs

A group structure is the most logical format for an after-school program because groups enable you to manage large numbers of children or teens. Groups also provide the best method to transfer skills from the program to real life (Brigman and Webb 2007). Groups can also strengthen a student's ability to learn (Sandler et al. 2005) and help students change unwanted or risky behaviors (Buhs et al. 2006). Unfortunately, not all groups are helpful. This is especially true with after-school groups (Roth et al. 2010).

Selecting a Group Format

As we move away from the traditional child care, homework help, recreational approach to after-school programming, the first question to ponder in developing an effective program is the following: *What type of group format should you use?*

Remedial programs. Many school-based after-school programs mostly include remedial work to improve scores on mandated tests. Such after-school programs may incorporate tutoring or administering practice tests. Although such programs may meet the need of schools to improve test scores, they do not fulfill both the academic and mental wellness needs of children and teens. Our goal is not just to improve mandated test scores; we want change for today and tomorrow. An example comes from a school where I conducted a short-term after-school program with the lowest scoring children in the first through third grade. I was given the children who were failing. I conducted my week-long *Camp Sharigan* (Clanton Harpine 2010a) reading clinic, which is a group-centered motivational program designed to get students excited about reading. I then conducted a once-a-week follow-up after-school program to target individual reading problems. At the close of the 6 weeks, the children who had participated in the *Camp Sharigan* treatment program out-scored the group who had not participated (Clanton Harpine 2005). Even though the children had improved over the 6-week period, they still needed more help. They were barely passing, but the school was not interested in extending the after-school program even though the students were showing definite signs of improvement. The school was mostly interested in improving test scores.

Prevention vs. remedial programs. Prevention programs provide knowledge and skills, but a prevention group is not a lecture session. A prevention program can work on academic needs as well as psychological needs. A preventive group may focus on preventing the outbreak of a problem (drug use with elementary students) or a prevention group may work to reduce the severity of an existing problem (academic failure) that could lead to even more severe, lifelong problems (drug addiction, unemployment, crime). A prevention group may use a psychoeducational format, a traditional counseling group, or a group-centered approach. One of the main advantages of a group-centered prevention program over a psychoeducational prevention program is that a group-centered program emphasizes both learning and counseling (Clanton Harpine 2008). Most psychoeducational programs stress social skills or other counseling principles but do not incorporate counseling and academic skill-building in the same program. Regardless of the approach, a prevention program seeks to bring about change, promote positive mental health and well-being, and use all aspects of group process, specifically group interaction and cohesion (Conyne and Clanton Harpine 2010). Everyone must be involved. If students are sitting and listening to a teacher talk as in a classroom, group interaction does not occur and without group interaction you do not have a prevention program. Although many programs use the prevention label, they are not actually prevention programs. Implementation is the key to success with any prevention program (Nelson et al. 2003).

Creating a successful prevention group for children. Children need programs that emphasize step-by-step procedures and active hands-on learning (Durlak et al. 2010b). Also, programs with a social skills component (Hill 2008) or content-oriented approach that also emphasizes interaction are more likely to succeed (Granger 2010; Hirsch et al. 2010). Groups are recommended instead of traditional one-on-one tutoring, because research findings show small groups to be more effective than one-on-one tutoring or classroom instruction in reading (National Reading Panel 2000). Until a National Institute of Child Health and Human Development study, one-on-one tutoring was considered the most effective technique with at-risk students (Invernizzi et al. 1997). An after-school program filled with hands-on interaction within a prevention-focused group-centered structure can fulfill both the academic and the psychological needs of children.

Creating a successful prevention group for at-risk teens. Violence begins in childhood. Learning emerges as one of the earliest stressors and potentially one of the leading causes of aggression and violence (Romero and Roberts 2003). A positive school experience can become a positive protective factor (Gloria et al. 2005). A negative, failing experience can become a lifelong sentence of continued failure, violence, and crime (Rodriguez et al. 2007). In 2009, approximately 607,000 students dropped out of school across the nation. The figures vary depending upon how the dropout rate is calculated, but the estimate that one out of every three students drops out of school is staggering. The dropout rate for African American and Hispanic youth is higher than for other ethnic groups, with Hispanic youth having the highest dropout rate in 2009 (National Center for Education Statistics 2011). Children who are retained are more likely to drop out of school (Orfield and Lee 2005). One out of every ten African American children repeats a grade in school; this is triple the number of Caucasian children and double the number of Hispanic children (National Household Education Survey 2007). At-risk teenagers need positive group experiences, a group which enables them to change unwanted behaviors and develop new positive behaviors in a safe protected therapeutic environment. A school classroom or a sports team is not necessarily therapeutic (Clanton Harpine et al. 2010) and may even be harmful, if negative behaviors are part of the group structure (Mahoney and Stattin 2000). Competition is not always healthy. It can be belittling. If your after-school program is to bring about positive change, you must develop a therapeutically supportive environment. If you are developing an after-school program for teenagers, you must definitely evaluate the academic needs of your students without overlooking the social problems of bullying (including cyber bullying), drugs (including cigarettes, alcohol), and other health risk behaviors. The importance of academic change with teens is emphasized by an example of a teenager who failed in reading for nine straight years in school. The school, the parent, and even the teenager did not think that the student would ever be able to learn to read. The student also had major behavior problems. The school considered that the behavior problems were of more immediate concern. Therefore, the school was addressing only behavior. When the teenager was placed in a group-centered prevention program in reading, the behavior problems disappeared once the student learned to read. Children and teenagers need both academic and social skills training.

Group-centered after-school prevention programs. Group-centered prevention programs for children and teens focus on learning as well as counseling. Typically some aspect of academic change in order to prevent academic failure, grade retention, and eventually prevent students from dropping out of school early is a major component of a group-centered prevention program. Since students spend the majority of each day at school, academic success plays an important role in healthy development and well-being. Group-centered after-school prevention programs emphasize intrinsic motivation (internal motivation), a positive atmosphere, active hands-on learning, structured skill-building activities, social skills training, creative group-centered therapy techniques, and group process that stresses positive interaction and cohesion.

Groups can help at-risk students. For the past 4 years, I have directed the *Reading Orienteering Club*, a group-centered after-school program focused on preventing reading failure. Each year, the children participating have shown academic improvement in reading (Clanton Harpine 2006, 2007a, 2010c, 2011b, 2012; Clanton Harpine and Reid 2009b). Some children have advanced two grade levels in 1 year. Others have needed more than 1 year in the program in order to make significant progress. This point is exemplified by two brothers who participated in my after-school reading program. They were both beginning readers and had been diagnosed by the school as having attention problems in class (ADHD). At the end of the year, one brother advanced two grade levels in reading; the other brother, although he improved, was still struggling. Each child is different and arrives with their own set of special needs. The key is to develop a successful group format (group-centered prevention) and then within that format build in individuality so that each student's needs can be incorporated.

Advantages of a group-centered format. A group-centered after-school program can become a safe group where children and teens can learn to manage the stress that is bombarding their lives and learn the skills to correct academic problems or failure. Research shows that group interventions can improve a student's ability to learn and overall mental wellness (Brooks-Gunn 2003; Sandler et al. 2005; Slavin 2002). Therefore, as we create the group structure for our after-school program, we want to stress academics and skill-building as well as the healing power of working together in a positive, supportive group. We will talk more in Chap. 2 about special learning needs and accommodations which might need to be built into your program. For now, we will lay the groundwork for organizing the group.

Step 1: Establishing the Focus of Your After-School Program

For each chapter in this book, I offer a step-by-step design procedure for developing a group-centered after-school prevention program. First, I present a list of questions with space for you to add your design ideas. Second, I present a design example showing how I answered these questions when I designed my *Reading Orienteering*

Club program. Each design step matches the theoretical concepts discussed in the chapter and fits the step-by-step procedure needed to design an effective year-long program. The purpose of the design example is to help clarify the questions and show the design process involved in developing a group-centered after-school prevention program.

Questions

What type of after-school group will you organize?

What type of problem will you seek to change? Academic? Psychological?

How many students will participate in your program? How will you select participants? Will you consider cultural and gender differences? What ages will you include? How will you organize for different ages?

Where will your group meet?

How many days a week will you meet? How many hours a day? How many months will you meet (9 months in accordance with the school schedule or a full year with a summer program)?

Will you have paid or volunteer staff? How many staff members?

Step 1, Design Example

Type of after-school program. I have chosen to organize a group-centered after-school reading program for first- through third-grade children. I am combining first-through third-grade children into one program because research shows that such a combination of ages provides a stronger group mentoring focus and stimulates motivation (Clanton Harpine 2011a, b). I will use learning centers with hands-on projects to provide intrinsic motivation and stimulate learning. Step-by-step instructions at learning centers will not only increase reading comprehension and problem-solving skills but also allow for the variety of ages and instructional needs that students will bring to the program. Learning centers will allow me to individualize instruction and also include one-on-one tutoring where needed. The group structure will give me the therapeutic setting that I need for the children. Learning centers provide a flexibility that a direct instructional focus (classroom teacher teaching a small group) cannot provide.

Problem. Reading is my selected problem. I'll talk more in Chap. 2 about why I chose reading as the academic problem that I wish to incorporate into my prevention program. Group-centered prevention works with any academic focus: math, history, science, or a combination of ideas. I have chosen reading because I work with an at-risk population, and it is impossible for them to succeed in other subject areas if they cannot read. My program will be a free program with open enrollment to all children (1st–3rd grade) in the community.

Students. My after-school program combines 20–30 first through third graders. In my research (Clanton Harpine 2005), I found this age combination to have many advantages. For example, third-grade children who were failing and struggling to learn to read did not feel intimidated working alongside first- and second-grade children because there were so many different age levels that even the children soon forgot who was reading at which level. Also, second and third graders who were beginning to read were very motivating to first graders. My research also demonstrated that the inclusion of fourth graders was not a good age combination (Clanton Harpine 2011a, b). I have found that children and teens work together best in a span of approximately third-grade levels (1st through 3rd, 4th through 6th, 7th through 9th, and 10th through 12th). You may choose to include sixth graders with middle school and ninth graders with high school teens, but I actually find that neither sixth graders nor ninth graders work well in such groupings. We also want to keep in mind the socioeconomic and cultural background of the group participants. According to research, gender differences are not significant in the design of your after-school program; everyone needs acceptance and a sense of accomplishment. Therefore, I do not need special adjustments in my program for males or females. Instead, I will stress understanding and acceptance for everyone.

Facilities. My program will be community based and sponsored by a church. It will be a nonreligious program. The church will simply be providing financial support and classroom space. We will use a combination of eight classrooms at the church (all situated on the same hallway). Children will move from classroom to classroom as they work at eight different learning center workstations. My program will be a very active, hands-on, group-focused, 9-month prevention program that focuses on reading, writing, and spelling. Eight classrooms will provide space for 30 children to move freely from station to station and work collectively in small groups. Age-appropriate tables and chairs in the church classrooms will provide ample work-space. The children rotate from room to room working at each of the eight learning center workstations. To work with more than 30 children, I would need to increase my classroom space. You never want to overcrowd. Overcrowding increases frustration; increased frustration increases behavior problems.

Schedule. My program will meet twice a week for 2 hours each session. The sessions will be very intense skill-building sessions. We will only meet twice a week because of staffing and budget constraints. The 2-hour sessions will be completely devoted to reading skills and group counseling in an interactive group setting.

Staff considerations. Staff and budget may be two primary concerns which determine how large or small a program you plan to design. You want to make sure that you have an adequate size staff to work with the children or teens in your program. My curriculum is designed with eight learning center workstations. Therefore, I try to work with a staff of at least ten volunteers. Do not overlook the role that volunteers can play as staff. I personally have college students work as tutors in my after-school program as part of a university classroom service-learning project. Community volunteers also work in the program. Learning centers with detailed instructional curriculum will allow me to rely on a volunteer staff rather than requiring a trained paid staff. A trained paid staff would be ideal but is not feasible at this time; therefore, I will design my curriculum to accommodate the instructional and psychological needs of my children and the financial constraints of my budget. My volunteers need only to help the children read and follow the learning center instructions. The program (learning centers) does the teaching. The volunteers offer one-on-one assistance.

Real-World Applications

At the end of each chapter, there will also be a section entitled, *Real-World Applications*. This section will have an observation assignment for you to go out and perform. This observation assignment is designed to help you in designing your own after-school program. A list of questions is also included to help you think ahead and troubleshoot for potential problems. At the close of this section, I will present a ready-to-use learning center workstation example demonstrating how to write learning center workstation instructions to include the theoretical principle being discussed in that chapter. The learning center example shows how to write learning center instructions for your students.

Observational Extensions

Go to observe an after-school program. On one side of a piece of paper, write down the problems that you see. On the other side of the paper, write down the successful aspects of the program. Why do you think the problems exist? Causes? What can be done to alleviate these problems?

Troubleshooting Checklists for Organizing a New After-School Program

1. What accommodations will be made for diversity among group members? Remember, the needs of the children always come first. Make sure that you have parents sign a parental permission form for the children to attend your program and fill out and sign a health form for each child or teenager.
2. What kind of budget do you have to work with? Will the budget meet the needs of your group? How will you make adjustments?
3. Are your building and facilities adequate? Do you need to sign a contract for use of the building space? Is there a cost? Restrictions?
4. Is your program free or do you charge a fee? Do you have a sliding scale for those who might need financial assistance?
5. Is your staff adequate for the number of children you wish to include in your program?
6. How many days a week is your program to meet? What hours?

A Ready-to-Use Group-Centered Learning Center Intervention, Designing a Learning Center to Meet the Cultural Needs of Your Participants: The Hat Cat

The example provided for this chapter stresses meeting the needs of your students. This example shows how to write learning center instructions for a variety of ages and different cultures. Each of the learning center examples given in this book talks about reading (that is my after-school program focus). I think demonstrating the writing of learning center instructions from one perspective (reading) and for one age group (1st–3rd) will be more helpful in showing how to pull the principles of group-centered prevention together in a year-long after-school program because these programming ideas come from an actual program and have been proven to work. These same principles can be applied to math, history, or science. I have chosen reading as our example because it is universal for all ages and for all areas of the country.

Over the years I have worked repeatedly in an inner-city Hispanic community after-school program for immigrant children. This program encourages children to learn English as quickly as possible. This sample learning center workstation shows how you might write learning center instructions for a bilingual community. This is a workstation written for first graders or children who are just beginning to read English words. The instructions are presented in English because a beginning reader is not able to read at the level in which instructions must be written; therefore, the instructions are intended to be read to the child by the workstation helper. Bilingual middle school and high school students often work as workstation helpers when I work in the Hispanic community and can give the instructions in Spanish when needed. This example also demonstrates what I mean by the term *vowel clustering* (Clanton Harpine 2010b). There are many different approaches to clustering vowel sounds. The approach that I use focuses on learning vowel sounds in clusters, regardless of what letters are used to make that vowel sound. Children in my program start with the beginning short *ă sound* and are able to read a story within the first week. Traditional early vowel reading books sold commercially combine too many vowel sounds together in one story for beginning readers. For example (traditional approach): *Tom has a big red ball. Tom ran to the red ball.* In these two sentences, eight different vowel sounds are introduced. Beginning readers cannot learn that many vowel sounds at one time; therefore, I teach vowel sounds in clusters. Clustering is in keeping with how the brain organizes and assimilates information which thereby increases the child's ability to decode and encode words (Keller and Just 2009). Vowel clustering means to simply teach words by vowel sound rather than by letter. For example, there are seven different vowel sounds for the EA vowel combination: break, heart, hear, search, sneak, head, and bear (does not include EA as a silent letter as in *beautiful* or *beau*). If the child knows that there are seven different sounds for the EA vowel combination, then the child can sound out and test those different sounds when the child encounters a word that they do not know. When we read, we say sounds, not letters; therefore, it is more logical to teach reading by learning sounds. This example also includes the term *capturing tricky words*. I use this phrase throughout all of my programs. Instead of saying, "you missed the word" or "that is incorrect," I say, *capture tricky words*. You will also notice that I do not introduce the words being used in a story in a reading list or teach the children keywords before asking them to read. Children can often remember or memorize a few keywords from a reading list. Then, instead of actually reading new words in a story, they are simply recalling words that they just practiced. If we want children to truly learn to read, we must teach them to sound out words without picture cues or pre-taught keyword lists. In writing this example, I have also used the learning center workstation format that I use in my *Reading Orienteering Club* program. This step-by-step format is easy for the children to follow. I use compass points in my program (N, E, S, W) to direct the children to all eight learning centers. Notice that because I have written this learning center workstation to be used in a bilingual community, I have written the story in both English and Spanish. Children who are just beginning to learn to speak English sometimes do better if they are allowed to read the story in Spanish for comprehension. Therefore, the option is provided. This does not mean that children will only read the story in Spanish. The Spanish translation is offered only to help in comprehension. Challenge steps are offered in my program for students who are ready to take the next step. Not all children will be ready for the challenge step.

THE HAT CAT

Step 1: We are going to read a story today. Reading a story is just as easy as reading a list of words. When you read, sound out each letter and then put the sounds together to form a word. Never guess. Guessing is not reading, and besides, when we guess, we often guess wrong. So, let's sound out the words and READ.

Step 2: Today, we are practicing the short ă *sound* in the word *at*. When we have only one vowel in a syllable, that vowel usually uses the short vowel sound. So, look for our short ă *sound* as in the word *at* in each word that we read today.

Step 3: Read: *bat, trap, van, map, add, sap*. If you captured any tricky words from the list, remember to use the *4-steps* that we have learned and practice your captured words: (Step 1) always say the letter sounds (say the word out loud) and spell the word, (Step 2) give a definition, (Step 3) use the word in a sentence, and (Step 4) write the word correctly.

Step 4: Now, let's read our story. Remember if you capture any tricky words in the story, use the *4-steps*.

THE HAT CAT

A black cat had a black hat.

The hat sat at a mat.

A tan rat sat in the black hat.

The cat spat at the rat.

The rat ran fast.

Step 5: Once you have finished the story and captured any tricky words (don't forget the *4-steps*.), answer the questions. If you need help answering questions, read the story in Spanish.

1. What color was the hat?
2. What happened to the rat?

Spanish version:

El Gato Sombrero
Un gato negro que tiena un sombrero negro.
El sombrero estaba sentado sobre un tapete.
Un raton bronceado sentado en un sombrero negro.
El gate le escupio al raton.
El raton corrio rapio.

Step 6: You may choose to either work the challenge step or go to the next station. Good job today.

ARE YOU READY FOR A CHALLENGE?

Challenge Step: Now, it is your turn. You are the author. Write a story using only short ă sound words. It's harder than you think, but you can do it. Remember, you are only allowed to use short ă sound words as in the word at. Of course, you may need to add the, on, a, or in, as I did in the story above. Even though we are writing a silly story, we do want all of our sentences to be grammatical. Have fun.

Chapter 2
The Group-Centered Approach

Two students enrolled in a group-centered after-school reading program at the same time. They were both 9 years old, but neither one could read. Neither student even knew the consonant or the vowel sounds. One student had been diagnosed with dyslexia; his parents were college graduates who tried desperately to help him at home. He also received special tutoring at school for dyslexia but was still reversing letters and trying to read from right to left across the page. The student was convinced that he would never learn to read. The second student came from a low socioeconomic neighborhood, single-parent home. The parent could not read and the child was convinced that he too would never learn to read. Unfortunately, this student had been exposed to cigarette smoke, alcohol, and crack cocaine by his mother during pregnancy. The student showed cognitive processing problems typical with prenatal drug use. The Reading Orienteering Club after-school program is a year-long program. At the end of the year, the first student (diagnosed with dyslexia) was reading beginning chapter books, first-grade level, and beyond. The second student (prenatal drug exposure) could read a vowel-clustered story at the pre-primer level, but was still struggling. How could the same program, same time, same location, yield totally different results with two different students? Does it mean that there is something wrong with the program?

Even though prevention programs measure success in terms of the degree of change that a program produces (Kulic et al. 2004), change will not always be the same for every student. This is still true for a group-centered prevention program, and it does not mean that your program is a failure. One of the major advantages of the group-centered approach is that it enables you to individualize instruction in a group setting. We must remember that students are individuals. They bring to the after-school program their own individual needs, problems, and learning styles. Some children will need more time than others to learn the same material. The group-centered approach enables you to design an after-school program which gives students the

E. Clanton Harpine, *After-School Prevention Programs for At-Risk Students:*
Promoting Engagement and Academic Success, DOI 10.1007/978-1-4614-7416-6_2,
© Springer Science+Business Media New York 2013

time and support that they need in order to learn and change their behavior. The key is to make sure that every child is indeed improving, even if that improvement is sometimes much slower than others in the group.

That two students lack reading skills does not mean that they have the same learning needs or problems. No two students, not even identical twins, learn the same way or in the same time span (Segal 2000). Both of the students in our opening example definitely needed help, but they had two different learning styles and problems. The group-centered approach allows you to work with both of these students in the same after-school group without having to pull students out of your after-school program and place them in special groupings. The group-centered approach is more than just a group that meets after school. The group-centered approach creates for you an after-school program that meets the individual needs of all students.

The Need for Individualized Instruction

Public schools offer a one-size-fits-all approach to learning. Even when they use diversified strategies and learning adjustments made for special needs, schools still only offer one method for learning (Riggs and Greenberg 2004). Students need more. The one-size-fits-all approach to learning and demand for documented change through mandated testing have destroyed teaching and learning as they should be conducted (Blaunstein and Lyon 2006). Numbers—test scores—do not always accurately measure student learning (Sternberg et al. 1997). Therefore, we want to look at individual change. We want to evaluate each student in our program as an individual learner. We do not want to compare one student's progress to another; we want to stay focused on the individual. Schools often talk about diversity and diversified learning, but I like to use the term "individualized learning" because we must continuously remind ourselves that students are distinct individuals. No two students are alike, and no two students learn or respond to learning interventions in the same way. We must not just diversify education and categorize students into groups. We must instead individualize their education.

Although research tells us that children learn how to read better when they work in small groups, I have a student who has only been able to learn new vowel sounds and vowel clusters when I work with him one on one. Yes, he is definitely benefiting from his participation in my *Reading Orienteering Club*, but he is only able to learn a new skill through a one-on-one approach. His social skills have improved from group involvement; his group behavior has totally changed for the better; his interactive skills have improved; he is much more motivated, and his ability to work with others in a group has greatly improved. Involvement in a group-centered program has significantly contributed to the student's overall improvement, but he still needs one-on-one teaching strategies to learn a new vowel sound or vowel cluster. The group-centered approach can provide this individualized learning opportunity through learning centers that include volunteer helpers at each workstation.

Individual Learning Needs

Every single student in your after-school program is an individual. Each one has distinct learning needs. We must understand our students' specific needs and develop a way to meet each and every individual need. We cannot simply organize after-school groups and just expect learning to take place automatically. The group is our medium for change. The group-centered approach is our tool for bringing about group and individual change.

Learning disabilities. Ten percent of children in the United States have a learning disability. A learning disability is neither a form of mental retardation nor an emotional disorder. A learning disability is a neurobiological disorder marked by how the brain processes and stores information. Low socioeconomic status, poverty, environmental influences, or cultural and/or acculturation problems do not cause learning disabilities. We do not know the exact cause of learning disabilities. We do know that learning disabilities are not caused by laziness or a lack of intelligence. Such famous people as Albert Einstein and Walt Disney were said to have learning disabilities. There seems to be a genetic or a hereditary link with learning disabilities, and there is a definite link between learning disabilities and how the brain develops. Most children with learning disabilities can succeed if they get proper instruction. Neither direct instruction in the classroom nor even computer-based learning seems to be effective with many students who struggle with learning disabilities (Slavin 2002). Hands-on learning and positive interactive groups seem to work better (Graham and Harris 2003). Students with learning disabilities need a program that can help them reorganize, retrain, and in some instances, as research has shown, generate new brain cells through intensive skill-building training sessions (Draganski et al. 2006). The group-centered approach allows you to individualize your teaching strategies to meet the specific needs of each student.

Prenatal drug effects. It has been estimated that about 475,000 newborn babies born every year have been exposed to crack cocaine; such exposure causes a variety of developmental deficits (Goldschmidt et al. 2008). The brain begins to form almost from the minute of conception. By the fourth week, the brain makes up almost 50 % of the embryo's total size. By week five, the brain has brain waves and produces about 100,000 neurons every minute (Nelson and Bosquet 2000). An infant is born with between 100 and 200 billion neurons. Such neurons and the connections between these neurons are what enable the child to learn (Merzenich 2001). Anything and everything consumed by the mother during pregnancy affects the development of these neurons and their connections. Any kind of aspirin or ibuprofen taken during pregnancy affects the development of the neurons in the unborn child's brain. Any kind of drugs or medications, even birth control pills taken by the mother before she realizes that she's pregnant, can have a harmful effect. Illegal drugs are even more dangerous because we do not know the strength, purity, or substances with which they are mixed. "Crack" cocaine, for example, can cause a lower IQ level, leading to problems with language development, and cause difficulties in comprehension, expressing ideas, hearing, and attention (Lewis et al. 2004). Any amount of alcohol, even as little as one ounce of wine or beer, can damage the unborn fetus's brain, particularly affecting verbal skills, attention, and cognitive processing (Cornelius et al. 2002). Nicotine reduces oxygen levels, and even secondhand smoke can damage the unborn child. Marijuana usage during pregnancy can cause the child to have problems later in spelling, reading, and comprehension (Goldschmidt et al. 2004). I call it simply SAD, because smoking, alcohol, and drugs make many children start life and school with a disadvantage, and it truly is SAD when you remember that prenatal drug damage can be completely prevented. This is as true for wealthy suburban neighborhoods as for low socioeconomic communities.

Autism. Autism spectrum disorder (ASD) is actually a complex range of neurodevelopmental disorders. A milder form of ASD known as Asperger's syndrome is more common among students identified by the schools. Most students with ASD have some degree of social impairment (trouble communicating, especially with others in a group) and sometimes show signs of repetitive or stereotypical type behaviors (Ozsivadjian and Knott 2011). We do not know what causes autism. ASD seems to affect more males than females, but there is not a cultural, ethnic, or socioeconomic link. The needs of students with ASD will vary greatly; therefore, it is impossible to prescribe a specific program or treatment. Structured group involvement does seem to help improve social skills (Koegel et al. 2012). For example, when a student diagnosed with ASD first arrived at my after-school program, he would not sit with the other students, did not want to work in the same room as other students, and would not let anyone touch him—not even to put on a name tag. After a few months in the program, he was moving from learning center to learning center, sitting in a chair beside others at the table, and even giving hugs to the staff when he arrived. After 2 years in the program, he began making friends, talking with other children. He has applied more effort to the task of reading. He even completed, without special assistance, a pop-up book about traveling to the moon. He traveled around the room to all eight workstations and completed each task. To make his pop-up book, he had to cut out and decorate a paper rocket with captured words, write two sentences on facts that he learned about the moon, and then write a story to go with his book. The project also includes fine motor skill development because the children are required to trace patterns and cut out the pieces for their pop-up book. Fine motor skill development is one of this student's major problems; so completion of this project was a gigantic step forward for this student. Today, his actions in a group are much different than when we first met. He even talks about "his friends." A group-centered structure helped to reduce this student's anxiety, enabling him to begin learning to work with others. Such changes in group behavior would not have been possible in a one-on-one tutoring situation; a group-centered structure was essential.

Attention deficit hyperactivity disorder (ADHD). ADHD is the most common neurobehavioral disorder diagnosed for children (Castle et al. 2007). The number of children diagnosed and prescriptions for stimulant medications are increasing daily (Bryant et al. 2003). In your after-school program, you will most likely have several children who have been diagnosed by the schools as having ADHD. I will not, in this book, enter the debate on whether medical or nonmedical intervention is best. All engaged in the treatment of ADHD support the need for nonmedical interventions to improve impulsive and distractive behavior in the classroom, interactions with peers, reading and math failure, and parent and family relations (DuPaul and Weyandt 2006). I strongly encourage parents to try structured non-medical interventions before trying medication. Every child is different, but with all drug therapies there are risks. To me, it makes sense to try nonmedical interventions first. Children diagnosed with ADHD need programs that emphasize step-by-step procedures and active hands-on learning (Jensen et al. 2007; Trout et al. 2007). Working in a group gives children diagnosed with ADHD the opportunity to learn and test new behaviors in a supportive group (Strayhorn 2002). The group-centered approach provides the structure, cohesive support group, and active hands-on learning interventions needed by children who have difficulty controlling their actions.

How the Group-Centered Approach Meets Individual Learning Needs

A group-centered prevention program stresses improving group behavior, enhancing peer and group interactions, and reducing academic failure. The group-centered approach can provide a strong supportive learning environment in which students can work and learn without the fear of rejection, but your after-school program must also teach organizational skills, problem-solving, and ways to deal with frustration. It must help children foresee the consequence of their actions and learn ways to control impulsivity, deal with distractions, acquire group skills, and change behavioral problems while incorporating new approaches to learning (Chard et al. 2002; Simonsen et al. 2010). Learning centers in a group-centered structure can help bring all of these variables together.

An example can be taken from the *Reading Orienteering Club*. This hands-on program encourages children to organize and assemble projects using a step-by-step process. The value of step-by-step instruction is well documented (DuPaul and Stoner 2004). For example, the children travel around to each learning center making and collecting word strips for the words learned that day. These reading strips are then attached as legs to a paper *Andy the Ant* puppet. The children organize and keep track of the pieces for their puppet as they travel from station to station. This is an important task for all children but especially children who struggle with distractibility and organization. They follow the step-by-step procedures to assemble their puppet. This lets the children practice personal organizational skills and group problem-solving as they figure out how to put the puppet together. They get lots of practice coping with frustration and controlling impulsive actions. Children are also able to see the consequences of their actions when they try to jump ahead and not follow directions correctly. Once the puppet is assembled, the children work together in teams to present a puppet play using their puppets. This type of hands-on learning center project provides practice with group skills and opportunities to monitor individual behavior. Children learn the vowel cluster and phoneme awareness skills they need in order to improve in reading and the social skills needed to work successfully with others in a group through one single project. This is the group-centered approach: focusing on individual needs while working together in a group and taking advantage of the therapeutic power of group process. Your program must meet the needs of all participants, not just a few. It is not easy to design a program that meets everyone's needs, but the group-centered approach for after-school programming can help you attain this goal.

How to Set Up and Develop a Group-Centered After-School Program

Designing or selecting the curriculum for your after-school program is one of the most important steps in the program development process. As explained earlier, simply buying an evidence-based program will not guarantee your success; therefore, we will focus on writing our own group-centered program. A group-centered program combines learning and counseling, but at this point in the design process, we will focus on developing the academic focus first. We will discuss how to incorporate the therapeutic aspect in Chap. 3. It is important to learn the group-centered approach one step at a time so that we do not delete any of the essential components of the group-centered method.

We'll begin by examining the problem that you selected in Step 1: *What type of problem will you seek to change?* As already discussed, I chose reading and will therefore use reading as my example.

The group-centered approach uses only program packets. Instead of having an outline for the program or a list of objectives, a program packet provides exactly what is said or done in the program. Everything is included in the program packet. The director of the after-school program simply opens the packet and lays out the booklets when they're ready to use the program. The packet includes learning center instructions, games, stories, patterns, and puppet plays, everything that is needed to run the program. The person in charge of the after-school program does not have to interpret the program or create materials for the program. The packet is complete. Using a ready-to-use program packet helps to ensure that both the hands-on at-risk teaching methods and the motivational group counseling techniques are used correctly because they are written into the learning center workstation booklets.

If you are using learning centers as we are in our program design in this book, your program packet will be your collection of learning center workstation directions and information for participants. Therefore, our next step is to learn how to write and set up a group-centered learning center.

Step 2: Designing a Learning Center to Bring About Academic Improvement

Identify the academic problem you wish to change. Why is the academic problem important for your students?

How will you bring about change? How will you use a group-centered approach?

How will you measure change?

What group techniques will you use?

What teaching strategies will you implement?

What kind of motivational strategies will you use?

Will you include communication strategies to help improve oral and written communication?

How will you implement your program?

What are the advantages of your program plan? What are the disadvantages?

What kind of curriculum will you use? What are the advantages of writing your own curriculum?

How often would your program meet?

Do you have a theme for your program? How will that theme be incorporated throughout the year-long program?

Develop a format for your learning center workstations. Be consistent. Develop a format that can be used throughout the year so that the students become familiar with the format that you are using.

Step 2, Design Example

Academic problem. Reading failure is the problem that I have chosen to change through the *Reading Orienteering Club* after-school group-centered prevention program. Reading is an important academic concern because learning to read is essential for success in life. Sixty percent of children in the United States have trouble reading, 20–30 % say reading is the most difficult task they must learn in school, and 38–40 % never learn to read (Lyon 1998). According to the *Nation's Report Card*, 40 % of all fourth-grade children read below grade level (National Assessment of Educational Progress 2009). This is not a new problem, and there has not been a significant improvement in reading scores in 2011 (National Center for Education Statistics 2011). Reading failure is rampant and continuingly unchecked. Children struggling to read in the first grade begin to show a decline in self-efficacy (belief that they can read) by the middle of the year, but 90–95 % improve if effective instruction begins before the end of first grade (Lyon 1998). Unfortunately, without effective instruction, 75 % of the children who fail to learn to read in first grade never learn to read (Lyon 1998). Research supports four causes for this failure: lack of phoneme awareness, low comprehension, lack of motivation, and the classroom teaching approach (Lyon 2002).

Plan for bringing about change. My design will emphasize the group-centered approach incorporating individualized instruction through a therapeutic group setting. Working in a group can be an excellent way to help children who have trouble controlling their actions learn to work in a group environment. I used a group painting session to help teach individual and group control. Everyone sat around the table in a circle with the painting in the center. Everyone was allowed to paint but only one person at a time; no one was left out, but children were called on to paint (flowers or trees) by how well they modeled the desired behavior of waiting quietly for a turn. No reprimands or punishments were issued, only praise as each child took a turn. This soon became an accepted routine and even the most fidgety students soon learned to sit quietly for a turn. Sometimes the children received specific assignments of what to paint: six blades of grass, three trees, or a specific flower. Each simple painting skill was demonstrated for each child.

Skill in painting was not the objective. The goal was to make a puppet stage of which the children could be proud. Some children might find it difficult to control their actions while painting without an enforced group structure, and the group-centered approach proved helpful for developing group control strategies. The day ended with free time after the structured painting session. Members could paint whatever they chose as long as they shared with others. Free time helped to release stress after the controlled activity.

Measuring change. As I gather together the students who will participate in my after-school program, I need to conduct a pretest to determine their skills and abilities at the start of my program. I also need to learn more about their background: What brain development problems and cognitive processing problems might students be bringing to the program? Are there any diagnosed problems or concerns? Student improvement must go beyond the after-school program to transfer back to the classroom (Duckworth et al. 2007), continuing into lifetime change (Obiakor 2001). It is important that the students are able to see and understand that they are improving. Pretesting, periodic follow-up testing, and a posttest at the end of the year are essential components of my after-school program. This is not so I can match a standardized test score or give a grade, which are negative measures of what the student has or has not attained. Instead, I want to chart improvement, regardless whether the improvement is slow or a huge leap.

Group techniques. I decided to create a fun, hands-on learning environment because the climate of a group is extremely important (Ogrodniczuk and Piper 2003), especially in a year-long after-school group (Nastasi et al. 2004). I definitely want to incorporate the therapeutic power of group process (Vacha-Haase and Thompson 2004), and I want the real-world environment where children problem-solve, test ideas, and incorporate new ways of interacting together (Finn et al. 2005). The group structure will also provide a setting in which at-risk children can resolve the everyday problems of childhood, such as seeking acceptance, coping with peer pressure, and learning to handle teasing and bullying (Gullotta et al. 2009).

Teaching strategies. I will use learning centers with step-by-step directions so that each student may work at their own individual pace and spend more time where they need the most help. There will be challenge steps at each learning center for those ready to tackle harder problems, and one-on-one guided tutoring for those needing extra help. I will stress interaction and cognitive skill-building (Granger 2010; Hirsch et al. 2010; Smith et al. 2010) to gain the most benefit from my group structure and my hands-on skill-building interventions. Word recognition is the first step to successful reading (Morris 1999); therefore, I want to stress word recognition skills and how words are composed by letter sounds. Such skills will help motivate students and also serve a protective function as we work step by step to rebuild their self-efficacy (Coie et al. 1993).

I adopted a vowel clustering approach for teaching beginning reading skills (Clanton Harpine 2010b). Decoding is said by many to be the most important skill needed for reading. My learning centers will stress encoding and decoding skills so that the children will learn how words are composed. Therefore, I will incorporate reading, writing, and spelling into my skill-building sessions. This will help students with learning disabilities and cognitive processing problems, because students with learning disabilities have trouble with phonological decoding, encoding, and fluency (Bryck and Fisher 2012).

Students with prenatal drug abuse show a definite need for intensive cognitive processing training. Research shows that the gray matter of the brain (where processing occurs) can be changed through skill acquisition (Torgesen et al. 2001). Neuroimaging studies also show that the white matter (the wiring or the connections in the brain which allow communication to, from, and within the gray matter) can be changed for poor readers through intensive instruction with phonological decoding skills (Draganski et al. 2006; Keller and Just 2009). Intensive instruction in encoding improves expressive writing (Gersten and Baker 2001). The white matter helps the brain to learn, but simply learning to read and write is not enough. Intense skills training can increase the connectivity or organization of fibers within the brain (Keller and Just 2009) and help at-risk students learn (Meyler et al. 2008). Therefore, I stress phonological awareness, encoding and decoding, vowel clustering, reading, writing, spelling, and comprehension.

Motivators. Intrinsic motivation, a positive atmosphere, and active hands-on learning will combine to create a fun, active, but also a very intensive skill-building program. Hands-on projects and themes will serve as motivators. My program will not use any kind of prize or reward system. My design will instead stress intrinsic motivation (internal desire not based on rewards or incentives), active hands-on learning, structured skill-building, anger management, cooperation, social skills, and group process with emphasis on interaction and cohesion. I will go into more detail on why I stress intrinsic (internal) rather than extrinsic (rewards) motivators in Chap. 4; my program plan will not include any form of extrinsic reward, food, candy, or prizes. I will use only intrinsic motivators.

Communication strategies. Action stories, puppet plays, group painting projects, and a pretend TV show will help the children practice oral communication skills. Structured skill-building activities, social skills training, step-by-step instructions for each task, cognitive processing skills necessary for learning to read, phonetic decoding skills, and group process techniques stressing interaction and cohesion at the learning center workstations will also stress small group work. The children will have an opportunity to work individually, in small groups, and as a total group. The variety of writing assignments (stories, pop-up books, and puppet plays) will also help students develop their writing skills.

Implementation. Regardless of how well designed a program may be, the outcomes will be less than intended if the program is poorly implemented (Durlak and Dupre 2008); therefore, I wanted to develop a means for enhancing implementation. I will use program packets (Clanton Harpine 2011a, b). A program packet contains ready-to-use hands-on learning center booklets which have step-by-step instructions for students and those directing the program. The benefits to ready-to-use program packets are obvious. Ready-to-use packets will insure that the programs are used as intended because workers and students will be reading directly from the learning center instructions. Program packets will also reduce preparation time for my volunteer after-school staff conducting the program.

Advantages and disadvantages of my program plan. Reading failure and retention increase the likelihood that a student will drop out of school before graduation (Nastasi et al. 2004). Reading failure has also been directly linked with classroom discipline problems, bullying and aggressive school violence, delinquency, adolescent substance abuse, and the development of depression and anxiety (Catalano et al. 2003; Greenberg et al. 2001). Dropping out of school increases the likelihood of turning to crime (Snowden 2005) and not being able to maintain adequate adult employment (Nelson et al. 2003). Reading failure is a lifelong problem. By reducing reading failure, I will help to prevent these problems from occurring with my students. Helping to change a student's life and improve their chances of attaining a better way of life as an adult is a definite advantage. One of the disadvantages is that group-centered program packets take time to write, but, once I have written the program packet, I can use it at multiple sites and for several years without the need to rewrite. Program packets also alleviate one of the major staff concerns with present-day after-school programs. Researchers have identified recruitment and retention of staff as a major concern. Many after-school programs have high staff turnover (Sheldon et al. 2010). My volunteers change every semester and sometimes every session. Program packets enable my after-school program to stay the same regardless of the staff working on a particular day. This will be particularly important in my program because I use volunteer college students.

Curriculum. The year-long *Reading Orienteering Club* curriculum is distributed as a program packet (Clanton Harpine 2013a). The curriculum consists of eight learning centers which can be used in any classroom or cluster of rooms with no prior setup. Everything is contained in eight workstation notebooks (program packet). All you need is the program packet with the learning center notebooks, basic school craft supplies (scissors, glue, paper), and a volunteer staff of at least ten people (eight learning center workers and two codirectors who float from room to room offering assistance where needed). The volunteers do not need special training because the teaching strategies and counseling interventions are written into the learning center instructions. The program packet contains ready-to-use booklets, not a manual, but the actual program, complete with learning center instructions. University undergraduate students and community volunteers (even middle school and high school students) serve as reading tutors in my program to assist the children at the workstations. Program packets make staffing my program easier because the university helpers are often drawn from several different college classes, and are not the same every week. The university students and community helpers are able to sit down, read over the instructions, and start to work with the children. I need a curriculum (program packets) that volunteers can literally walk in and use.

Schedule. My program will meet twice a week for 2-hour sessions after school. My program could easily meet 5 days a week, but our budget at this time will not support a 5-day program. The program packet is written to accommodate any combination of after-school sessions: twice a week or 5 days a week.

Theme. The first step in writing a ready-to-use program packet is to develop a theme. My theme for the *Reading Orienteering Club* is that of an explorer using a compass to chart their way through *tricky words*. I have North, East, South, and West compass signs in the hallway to direct the children to the different learning centers. I use *vowel clustering* throughout the year to take the children from the *short A vowel sound* at the beginning of the year to compound and multi-syllable words at the end of the year. There are *Word Master* projects which help the children master each vowel sound, and there are 12-session themes which help focus and motivate students to learn more about a particular subject, such as the ocean or outer space exploration. The children read stories and learn about the *ocean* while they are practicing the vowel sounds for the letter O. They paint a coral reef puppet stage and make an *Ollie Octopus* pop-up book. The story themes are fun and help the children apply the principles of *vowel clustering*. The learning center workstations teach the children each vowel sound, stressing encoding and decoding in order to help the children learn to read, spell, and write correctly. Students work at their own pace. Everyone starts at Step 1, and there is always a *Challenge Step* to encourage those who are ready to try something new.

Format. I continue using the compass points for the eight learning center workstations: North, Northwest, Northeast, East, Southeast, South, Southwest, and West. Since I use a cluster of rooms, I mark the rooms in the hallway with compass poles: North, East, South, and West. Everything is portable in my program because the rooms are used by other groups throughout the week. I distribute 3-ring notebooks to the rooms with corresponding compass designations. Craft supplies are distributed as needed or placed on a rolling craft cart for workers to gather. I use step-by-step instructions for each learning center and always include a challenge step. The children must choose to take the challenge step; it is not required. An example of my format page for each learning center station is as follows:

NORTH

Step 1:

Step 2:

Step 3:

ARE YOU READY FOR A CHALLENGE?

Challenge Step:

Real-World Applications

Observational Extensions

Go to the classroom, and observe students working on the academic problem that you wish to include in your after-school program. Do not go with the intention of copying what the teacher is doing. You want your program to be totally different from what the children do all day in school. Do take note though of what works with the children and what does not. Remember you are developing a hands-on program.

Troubleshooting Checklists for Organizing a New After-School Program

1. How many learning centers will you use?
2. Will you have a helper at each learning center?
3. Have you taken learning disabilities into account? How will your program design meet the needs of these students?
4. Are you working with children who have prenatal drug exposure? How will your design meet the needs of these students?
5. Will you administer a pretest? How will you measure progress throughout the year?

A Ready-to-Use Group-Centered Learning Center Intervention, An Example of How to Build Teaching Strategies into a Learning Center Format: I Am Happy

This is an example of an easy-to-use learning center workstation that stresses phoneme awareness, comprehension, intrinsic motivation, and a hands-on teaching approach. Everything needed is included at the workstation. The sentence is written on sentence strips, ready to lay out on a table or the floor, and included in the packet. The stack of cards distributed to the children are also printed on card stock and included in the packet. The word cards include apple, slice, cat, ice, sat, it, and take. The letters are intentionally not the same as in the sentence because I want the children to concentrate on the letter sound. They have practiced this in previous sessions; therefore, it would not be a new concept to them, just more practice. For example, *apple* could be matched to *am*, *happy*, or *have*. Each word uses the *short a vowel sound*, but uses different letters to create that sound. *Take* may not be matched to *have*, even though it uses *silent E*, because it uses a totally different vowel sound.

By playing the game, the children are being taught to read and analyze how words are composed—encoding and decoding. Matching letter sounds teaches phoneme awareness. All the volunteer worker needs to do is help the children read the directions and play the game. Giving an open-ended response to a question requires comprehension and assimilation of what that question means to the child. The fun nature of the game is intrinsically motivating. Hands-on teaching strategies not only teach phoneme awareness but also reinforce positive actions toward others (counseling) and teach proper group behavior (counseling) as the children work together to play the game. You will notice that the game requires children to list friendship traits, not names. You never want to have the children play favorites by identifying who they like as a friend. It's like choosing teams; someone is always left out or the last one to be mentioned. That is not what you want at all. Therefore, make sure that you do not write your learning center workstation directions in such a way that children could embarrass someone and could have one person chosen over another, that someone might laugh at someone else, or that someone in any way might hurt another's feelings.

I always include a challenge step, but the child must choose to take the challenge. Some children may not be ready for the challenge; for those who struggle with the initial vowel task, reshuffle the first cards and let them use the first deck of playing cards and match a different word. For those who want to take the challenge, help them work with the words or do the words together as a group: caterpillar, hideout, action, acrobat, interesting, and iodine. This learning center station teaches phoneme awareness, motivates children to learn, requires comprehension and understanding, and uses group interaction and hands-on teaching strategies. The children also practice working together as a group, reading out loud, and stressing positive thoughts and actions. This is an example of the group-centered approach. Volunteers really can walk in with the children, sit down, and use the learning center instructions in the packet to teach both academic and counseling strategies.

I AM HAPPY

Step 1: We have been working on vowel sounds for the letters A and I. Today, we want to play a game together using these two vowel sounds. The first rule is to remember that we are a team, and we always work together and include everyone in our game. No one is ever left out or laughed at. We work together and help each other.

Step 2: The second rule to remember is that we're matching vowel sounds, not letters. Remember to watch out for silent E. Sometimes it changes the preceding vowel sound and sometimes it does not. So be careful.

Step 3: The third rule in our game is that everyone reads the sentence, lays down a card next to the vowel sound it matches, and then fills in the blank with a positive friendship trait. For example, I would read the sentence: "I am happy to have a nice friend _____." I could fill in the blank by saying, "who shows they care, who smiles, who helps me, who is always kind, who likes to work together, who shares fairly," or something positive of that nature. Then, I'd match my card. If I had drawn the card with the word *apple* on it, I would match *apple* to *have* in the sentence. The word *apple* and *have* both use the same *short a vowel sound*. Remember, we are matching vowel sounds, not letters.

Step 4: Now that we know how to play the game, let's get started. Take the sentence strips from the packet and lay them either on a table or on the floor, wherever there is space. Make sure that the sentence reads: I am happy to have a nice friend_____.

Step 5: Place the word cards upside down and have everyone draw a card, just one. No, you may not trade cards. Once you have drawn a card that is the card you are to play the game with. Go around the circle; make sure that everyone gets a turn. And remember, there's a time to be funny and there's a time to share serious thoughts. This is a time to share serious thoughts; something you really feel. Only positive friendship traits count in this game. Work the challenge step or go to the next station. Thanks for playing the game nicely with others.

ARE YOU READY FOR A CHALLENGE?

Challenge Step: If you are ready for a challenge, take the challenge cards from the packet. The challenge cards contain multi-syllable words. Each challenge card matches a word in the sentence, but they are very tricky. Be careful. Work together. Help each other. Remember, we are a team, and we always help each other.

Chapter 3
Combining Learning and Counseling into One After-School Program

They were siblings, approximately 2 years apart in age. They were both enrolled in the Reading Orienteering Club. It was obvious from the first day that the mother showed partiality toward the younger child almost to the point of ignoring the older child. The older child was about three grade levels behind in reading. The mother stated, "I do not know what is wrong with that one." This was a middle class two-parent family, but the disparity between attention and treatment by the mother, while not the cause, most definitely contributed to the problems that the older child was experiencing.

Even when a child grows up in a two-parent family with a seemingly stable home life, a traditional family structure does not guarantee that a child will receive the necessary support and nurturing. Unfortunately, many children are suffering, and some of them will find their way to your after-school program. An after-school program that only stresses improved academic skills is not enough. The group-centered approach combines both learning and counseling.

Exactly what is counseling? Often, when people hear the word group counseling, they think of people sitting around in a circle of chairs talking or listening to someone give advice. Actually, you don't even have to be in a circle or sit in chairs; counseling is about learning new ways of behaving, feeling, and thinking (Broderick and Blewitt 2006). Counseling stresses helping people cope with everyday living and developmental problems (Gazda et al. 2001). The primary objective of counseling is to improve well-being and to bring about change (Posthuma 2002). A positive group experience can provide a child or a teenager with acceptance and a sense of belonging (Baumeister et al. 2003). A group-centered after-school prevention program can provide counseling and become a safe place to learn and a safe environment in which to interact with others, but simply giving positive reinforcement is not enough.

All too often we think that positive feedback is all that is needed, but with the group-centered approach, we will learn that group support must be more than just positive comments. The term self-esteem (feeling good about one's self) has been

E. Clanton Harpine, *After-School Prevention Programs for At-Risk Students: Promoting Engagement and Academic Success*, DOI 10.1007/978-1-4614-7416-6_3, © Springer Science+Business Media New York 2013

popularized and many have been made to believe that self-esteem holds the answer to all of our interpersonal problems (Larsen and Ketelaar 1991). Unfortunately, that is not true (Baumeister et al. 2005). Self-esteem will not help a student learn or change from failure to success. Positive reinforcement or boosting self-esteem will also not counteract negative family problems, peer group problems, or negative perceptions (Lauer et al. 2006). If you want to bring about change, you must offer more than just positive comments (Bandura 1995).

When we talk about adding a counseling element to the after-school program, we are talking about more than just positive comments and kindness. We are talking about adding an actual mental health component. When we use the term "mental health" in this book, we are not saying that by merely attending an after-school program a child or a teen who has been diagnosed with bipolar disease, schizophrenia, or other serious mental disorder will suddenly be cured. Severe mental health problems must be dealt with by a trained therapist, but many developmental problems and mental health issues such as anxiety and depression can be prevented or significantly reduced through early intervention in prevention programs (Herman et al. 2008). So, when we talk about mental health in this book, we are talking about the benefits to mental well-being from reducing stress, replacing negative perceptions with positive perceptions, rebuilding self-efficacy, controlling behavior, erasing failure, and learning to work effectively in a group with others. If we incorporate these mental health components into our after-school program, we can help improve the mental wellness of students (Huang et al. 2005) and prevent or lessen the severity of mental health problems (Fleming et al. 2004). To incorporate these mental health components into our after-school program, we must better understand the background and perceptions that students bring to the program.

Perceptions and Past Experiences

The negative influence of failure. Students often refuse to try in school because they are convinced that they will fail (Zimmerman et al. 1996). When students refuse to try because of fear, their fear stifles learning. A student's negative perception of their ability or lack of self-efficacy can actually lead to depression and psychological distress (Ward et al. 2010). If the student feels ostracized or labeled as a failure, the stigma of these negative interactions becomes intertwined with the student's self-concept (Brody et al. 2002). Before long, students begin to believe other's perceptions of their ability.

Two students joined my *Reading Orienteering Club* after-school program, both reading above their grade level. Their comprehension was good. Their enthusiasm and cooperation were excellent, but as I soon learned, neither student could spell—not even beginning pre-primer words. They were totally mortified whenever they were asked to write a sentence or to write a word. They were embarrassed and did not want anyone to notice that they could not spell. One student tried to hide. He was afraid the other children would laugh at him. A student's inability to control negative perceptions and negative interactions with others can have adverse effects on the student's mental health (Berking et al. 2008). Children and teens both antici-pate success or failure on the basis of their past experiences. If the student has suc-ceeded in the past, then the student expects to succeed, even in a new situation. If, however, the student has failed in the past or been made to feel like a failure, then the student is likely to fail because negative perceptions lead to failure.

Such perceived feelings of success or failure develop from the student's level of confidence (self-efficacy), from the actual skills the student has learned, and from the student's perception that they can perform as others do (Cantor et al. 1986). Negative self-efficacy or a perceived sense of failure can actually cause students to fail simply because they believe that they will (Bandura and Schunk 1981). As a young first grader explained to me one time, "I can't read. My mama can't read. My brother can't read. I don't read." Such negative feelings if they are allowed to go unchecked can lead to mental stress. Students who suffer from some form of mental stress are at a higher risk for discipline problems, bullying, delinquency, substance abuse, and failure in school (Greenberg et al. 2001; Miller and Shinn 2005; Nikulina et al. 2011). Erasing failure is one of the first and foremost tasks confronting any after-school program.

Multicultural considerations. If the students in your after-school program come from different cultural experiences, then you must take such cultural experiences into consideration as you design your after-school program. As children grow, develop, and progress through the acculturation process (the process of adjustment and change that occurs from living in a new culture), much of the stress in their life is centered on school, learning a new language, and developing their self-identity in a bicultural society (Edwards and Lopez 2006). Language proficiency is listed as one of the essential factors needed for successful acculturation and is also listed as one of the primary sources of stress for adolescents (Zea et al. 2003). Language and the inability to communicate contribute to perceived discrimination (Romero and Roberts 2003); perceived discrimination contributes to psychological stress (Moradi and Risco 2006).

The family can be either a positive or a negative influence (Brook et al. 2001). In Hispanic communities, particularly Mexican immigrant communities, success in school is viewed as an obligation (Lugo Steidel and Contreras 2003). Failure to meet this obligation creates stress and a sense of helplessness, and often even poses a threat to family integrity (Goldston et al. 2008). Parents often encourage education as the pathway out of poverty. Family expectations and a perceived sense of family obligation create a high degree of stress (Zayas et al. 2005) and often even the devel-opment of at-risk behaviors (Sale et al. 2005). It has been estimated that 75 % of the Hispanic children referred for psychiatric services also have language and reading problems (Toppelberg et al. 2006) and that 81 % of Hispanics read below grade level at fourth grade, the highest percentage of any ethnic group (Lyon 1998). Overall, a staggering 64 % of Hispanic students display reading skill deficiencies (Arnold and Doctoroff 2003). By improving academic abilities, we should be able to reduce acculturation stress, reduce dysfunctional behavior, increase school completion, and hopefully prevent later developmental mental health concerns (Pressley et al. 2007).

The influence of socioeconomic factors. Many students, particularly in inner-city, rural, and underserved communities, do not find school to be a positive experience. Students from at-risk communities often assume that they will not be able to learn or be successful in school (McWhirter et al. 2007). This leads to many of these students dropping out of school, securing low-income or often part-time employment, and eventually turning to crime (Twenge and Campbell 2002). Family conflict can be one of the most compelling stressors and eventual mental health problems for children and adolescents (Weissberg et al. 2003).

Nevertheless, students may also come from homes where education is sometimes considered to be unimportant or where parents may not even be able to read. Children from at-risk neighborhoods often start school at a disadvantage because they have not been exposed to the same learning opportunities as other students (Fredricks and Eccles 2006). Students from low socioeconomic neighborhoods rarely visit the community library, and even those who do visit the library frequently sit and play games on computers in the library rather than read a book. Reading is simply not stressed in many low socioeconomic communities. Students are often classified as failures because of inappropriate classroom behavior, inability to pay attention in class, lack of appropriate skills to start school, or sometimes just because they come from low socioeconomic neighborhoods with low academic expectations (McWhirter et al. 2007). Inappropriate or aggressive classroom behavior combined with academic failure typically leads to overall failure.

Many parents cannot afford private tutoring; therefore, when children fall behind in school, the decline is ongoing and unchecked; it often leads teens from low socioeconomic neighborhoods to drop out of school early. The expectation of failure increases the likelihood of failure (Deci et al. 1991) and risky behaviors (Nelson et al. 2003). As a young 7-year-old explained to me, "I don't need to read. I need people to fear me. They need to know I'm mean, and they'd better be scared." This young student lived in a drug-infested neighborhood where gang recruitment started at 5 or 6 years of age. The need to belong and be accepted (Baumeister and Leary 1995) is especially important for students who come from low socioeconomic households and at-risk neighborhoods. Gang membership is seen by many as more important than an education. If you are working with children or teens from at-risk neighborhoods, you need to be prepared for children who may or may not see an education as being important in their life. Your first step may be to convince them of the need for an education. As one teenager stated, "I don't need to worry about that stuff. I'm a singer. I'm *gonna* be famous. Make millions." Fortunately for this student, the group worker replied: "If you do not learn how to do simple math, how will you know if your agent is cheating you or not? If you can't read, how are you going to be certain that you're signing a contract that gives the money to you and not to someone else? If you're going to be famous, you'll definitely want to be able to read your contract and count your money." Children in low socioeconomic neighborhoods have access to fewer resources for learning, less parental support, but a higher likelihood of experiencing trauma, neglect, and stress (Nikulina et al. 2011; Noam and Hermann 2002). High stress can have a negative effect on brain development (Bryck and Fisher 2012). A strong academic skill-building program with a strong defined structure is helpful to students who come from very chaotic communities and families. If you incorporate hands-on learning techniques into your after-school program, you can help underachieving at-risk students master the skills necessary to perform successfully at grade level and increase their self-efficacy (Fall 1999). By rebuilding self-efficacy, you can help a student change their life.

Mental health issues with children and teens. Half of all medical health problems have a mental health component, and 1 in 10 children suffer from some form of mental illness (US Public Health Service 2000). Both children and teenagers spend the majority of each day in school. When students in school perceive that others classify them as failures, either teachers or classmates, such negative perceptions open the door for all kinds of developmental problems (Ward et al. 2010). Academic success is essential to mental health and well-being (Foorman et al. 2003; Rayner et al. 2001). Interventions and strategies that help students replace failure with success enhance a student's mental wellness (Ediger 2002). Every time a student is criticized or made to feel as if they are inadequate, their self-efficacy (belief that they can succeed or learn) is lowered (Vansteenkiste and Deci 2003). Yet, false praise will not help a student to learn (Baumeister et al. 2005). A successful after-school program must employ effective skill-building in order to rebuild a student's self-efficacy (Bandura 1997).

An after-school group-centered prevention program that focuses on academic learning and teaches group and individual social skills through group-centered counseling interventions can fill the need to reduce stress, to reverse negative perceptions, to offer acceptance and understanding, and thereby improve the mental wellness of its participants (Bandura 1998). Longitudinal research already shows that early intervention through prevention programs has been effective in reducing violence, underage drinking, teen pregnancy, disruptive behavior, and low achievement (Hawkins et al. 1999). Group counseling is one of the best prevention techniques being used in mental health because it enables children and teens to experience change in a group setting which easily translates back to real life (Hoag and Burlingame 1997). Prevention-focused activities which use positive group cohesion and supportive group interaction can create an environment in which healthy well-being can take root (Weissberg et al. 2003).

Does Your After-School Program Enhance Mental Wellness?

A college student volunteering in my *Reading Orienteering Club* after-school prevention program recently asked, "Why are we teaching reading? I thought that this was a psychology program. I'm a psychology major."

I often hear this question, and I always respond: You cannot have mental well-ness and psychological well-being, which of course is the goal of any psychologist, if your client is suffering from a sense of failure because they cannot read. Reading is one of the primary and basic necessities for better employment, and for a more satisfying standard of living. Mental wellness is dependent upon a person being able to successfully learn to read. To rebuild a person's self-efficacy and teach them to read, we must teach the basic skills necessary for learning to read. As Albert Bandura (1977) stated, you must teach skills if you want to bring about change in a person's life. Psychology is all about helping a person change their life and improve the way in which they are living. Reading is our catalyst for psychological change.

The reverse side of the coin is education majors come to me and say, "Is it really necessary to add in all of this counseling stuff? I just want to be a teacher; I'm not planning to go on into school counseling."

The truth is that you cannot separate academic learning and mental wellness. You simply cannot have one without the other (Greenberg et al. 2003). Your focus may not be reading as mine is, but the group-centered approach includes both coun-seling and learning. After-school programs provide an excellent opportunity to cul-tivate both learning and mental wellness. As you design your after-school program, make sure that you are including both counseling and learning.

A steel mill recently reopened and advertised their desire to hire local residents. They actually planned to give preference to those in the community because they wanted to help lessen the community's high unemployment rate. Unfortunately, they were unable to hire many of the local residents because the applicants could not read. The employer explained, "Even in a steel mill, you must be able to read the safety warnings." The local residents were very resentful of the "move-ins" who were brought in to fill the steel mill jobs. Such resentment fed directly into violence and community dissension.

You will need to choose your own catalyst for change and reason for developing an after-school program. My catalyst is reading. Regardless what you choose, edu-cation and mental wellness must be a part of any successful after-school program. Your program may not have a psychological base as reading does, but your program can incorporate positive counseling techniques which encourage and support healthy well-being and happiness. These are qualities we all seek and need.

Incorporating Mental Wellness into an After-School Program

Irvin Yalom, a noted group psychotherapist, states that there are 11 therapeutic fac-tors which we must incorporate into any group if we wish to bring about mental health, well-being, and psychological change. These factors are instillation of hope, universality, imparting information, altruism, recapitulation of the primary family group, development of socializing techniques, imitative behavior, interper-sonal learning, group cohesiveness, catharsis, and existential factors (Yalom and Leszcz 2005).

As we examine each of these therapeutic factors, I use examples from my program design showing how these factors relate to reading. You will want to relate them to your own program and your program's needs. These 11 therapeutic factors are essential in group counseling, regardless of the age of your students or the subject emphasis that you have decided to teach.

Hope. Everyone has an inner need to belong and be accepted by others in a group (Baumeister and Leary 1995). Academically, children and teenagers need to believe that it is possible for them to improve, make a better grade, or learn a new skill (Deci and Ryan 1985). Seeing improvement gives students hope. There is a strong correlation between academic failure, depression, anxiety, dropping out of school before graduation, unemployment problems, and tendency toward violence and crime (Hoglund and Leadbeater 2004). Improvement in academic skills helps to bring about improvement in mental health (Maugban et al. 2003). Skill-building gives students hope; therefore, skill-building is an essential element in any after-school program design because of both the academic and psychological needs of students (Lauer et al. 2006).

Universality. We are all very distinct individuals. We each have unique skills, talents, and unique personality traits that make us different from others; even identical twins are not completely identical (Segal 2000). We also share common fears. Since young children learn on a public stage, like the classroom (Adams et al. 1999), the fear of failure is an unfortunate working component of the school classroom. Working in a group program with other children or teens in an after-school setting often helps students realize that they are not the only ones who are struggling. We do not want students to group together and become complacent in failure; this too can happen. Instead; we want students to find support and understanding while they strive to learn and change. This feeling of acceptance encourages children to take a risk, to try. The group nature of a group-centered program shows ample examples of others working, of others trying, and even of others struggling.

Imparting information. All prevention programs teach new information or skills. The key to success with your after-school program is how you teach these skills. If you simply mimic the approach and technique of the school classroom, then you are doomed for failure. Children who fail to learn in the classroom at school using the traditional learning strategies and curriculum will not suddenly learn just because you take those same interventions and strategies and place them in a community-based after-school setting. Skill-building is essential (Bandura 1994), but the manner in which you teach these skills will determine whether your program is a success or a failure. Many after-school programs rely on completing homework sent from school, but such programs do not bring about academic change (Sheldon et al. 2010). Researchers found that homework does not in most cases lead to improvement at school academically, grades, or with standardized tests (Cooper et al. 2006). Parents like it when after-school programs concentrate on helping students finish their homework, but if the goal of your after-school program is to bring about academic improvement and change as well as mental wellness, then homework will not help you accomplish your goal. Homework does not teach; it simply adds to the frustration. When a child falls behind or is unable to keep up with the pace set by the teacher in the classroom, the child is embarrassed, confused, and begins to start down the road toward psychological destruction. Anxiety and depression can actually grow out of a sense of failure or from frustration over homework that the child does not know how to complete. A second grader came from school to an after-school program with a packet of 14 worksheets. The child was in tears, saying that she had to complete each of the worksheets or she would be in trouble with her teacher. Unfortunately, the child did not know how to work any of the worksheets. The worksheets represented a review of the concepts that the child never learned and still did not understand. The worksheets represented stress, failure, and negative perceptions. When taught the skills necessary to complete one of the worksheets, the child was all smiles, but it was impossible to teach 14 different concepts (represented by the 14 different worksheets) in 1 hour. Therefore, the child left the after-school program in tears and afraid to go back to school.

Altruism. Giving is therapeutic, but giving doesn't have to involve gift giving or money. Helping others helps us to feel better about our own situation in life. A gift of one's time is much better than a monetary or a tangible gift. This might include learning to work together as a team to accomplish a task, organizing community service projects, or just simply working alongside or encouraging someone who is struggling. Failure in school is perceived as a "negative event." For a young child in first grade, such failure can have disastrous psychological consequences (Herman and Ostrander 2007). Learning that others are not judging you or that others are willing to help you without assigning a grade can strengthen a student's willingness and desire to try harder.

Family, classroom, or peer group. Your after-school group will become a community-based entity which offers a separate peer group from the neighborhood or the school classroom. Your after-school group will take on almost a family-like structure. Remember, YOU set the standards for your program, not the students. At-risk students desperately need structure, especially structure that is consistently enforced. Again, do not fall into the self-esteem public school mindset. High self-esteem will not necessarily help a student learn or help a student's developmental wellness (Riggs and Greenberg 2004).

Social skills. Poor language skills lead to poor social skills and poor social functioning. Poor language skills also predict a lack of acceptance by peers, unless for acceptance into a dysfunctional group. Group interaction in a safe group setting within your after-school program allows students to test, develop, and refine social skills and behavior with others. A cohesive, interactive group creates a safe place to learn in a real-world-type situation and setting, but you must build this cohesive, interactive group structure into your program. It will not happen automatically.

Imitative behavior or modeling. Your after-school program can become somewhat of a reflective mirror through which children and teens may test their actions and the reactions of others to their actions. Positive modeling requires a positively cohesive, totally accepting, interactive group. Students who have difficulty learning are more likely to repeat a grade in school, to drop out before graduation, or to engage in violence, bullying, delinquent behavior, and substance abuse (Gottfredson et al. 2004). Failure leads to negative interactions; therefore, you must build opportunities for positive interactions into your program design (Zimmerman and Kitsantas 2005).

Interpersonal learning. Without interaction, there can be no interpersonal learning. Children and teens do not learn how to interact with others by sitting and watching a movie, listening to a lecture, role-playing, or being told how to interact with others. If you want to incorporate interpersonal learning, you must use group interaction. For any after-school prevention program to succeed, it must include group interaction and interpersonal learning. Group interaction means that each child is interacting with every other child. No one is ever left out.

Group cohesiveness. A positive group experience depends on how group process develops during group sessions. Cohesion becomes the spark which ignites change (Holmes and Kivlighan 2000), but many programs for children and teens do not stress interaction or cohesion, even though cohesion is important (Finn et al. 2005). Groups offer a unique therapeutic advantage (Fuhriman and Burlingame 1994); group members have the opportunity to be both helpers and seekers of help. This is particularly important for children struggling with a learning disability because they come face to face with others struggling with the same problems that they are facing. A group provides the members with acceptance and belonging (Hogg et al. 2004).

Catharsis. Catharsis implies the freedom to express both positive and negative feelings. Catharsis does not mean that you have the right to attack or hurt someone else or to hurt their feelings. Children and teens need to learn how to express their feelings without hurting others.

Responsibility. Yalom uses the term existential factors (Yalom and Leszcz 2005). For children and teens I like to refer to such factors as simply learning to accept responsibility for one's actions. I spend a lot of time talking about the consequences of your actions. I often find that at-risk students rarely think in terms of the consequences of a particular action. We all make choices in life, and sometimes life forces choices upon us. Yet, no matter whether we are rich or poor, live in a functional or a dysfunctional family, struggling or not struggling in school, liked or disliked by peers, there are still choices for us to make in life. The actions and choices we make often determine our happiness, well-being, and success in life. At-risk students often need help getting past the anger, blaming of others, self-pity, and frustration. When children who have struggled or failed are finally successful, their mental and psychological state improves (Slavin and Madden 2001). Failure, very simply, is a psychological problem as well as an educational problem because any time a student is classified as "slow" or as unable to learn, the student becomes stigmatized; such stigmatization hinders normal psychological development and prevents the individual from becoming a happy, healthy, and successful member of society (Adelman and Taylor 2006). If we can prevent failure, we will increase the student's chance for a happy, well-adjusted productive life (Bandura et al. 2001; Prilleltensky et al. 2001). Teaching responsibility and improving a student's potential for psychological well-being are most definitely within the ability of an after-school prevention program.

How to Build Mentally Healthy Counseling Interventions into Your Program

If we can create year-long after-school academic and therapeutic interventions that help students erase the stigmatizing effects of being labeled "a failure or at-risk of failing," then we will have made a psychological contribution to the health and well-being of students of all ages (McCall and Green 2004). If we can design after-school prevention programs that can be implemented in the community and conducted by volunteers with only minimal training, we have greatly multiplied the number of students that we can help (Linnenbrink and Pintrich 2002). Volunteers participating in service-learning projects in local high schools (Bradley 2005) and on university campuses (Kaye 2004) can offer a wealth of assistance to struggling children if such after-school programs use a curriculum that works with volunteers. Therefore, our next task is to write learning center workstations which support both the academic and psychological needs of the students in our after-school program. Work through the design questions below and write learning center directions for an activity which emphasizes the 11 therapeutic factors.

Step 3: Designing a Learning Center to Enhance Mental Health and Wellness

How will you work academic needs and counseling needs into the same program?

What types of psychological or developmental problems will you address?

How will you build counseling interventions into your academic skill-building sessions?

How will you bring about change in mental wellness?

How will you incorporate the 11 therapeutic factors?

Step 3, Design Example

Incorporating learning and counseling into the same program. I help children rebuild a positive self-efficacy (belief that I can complete a learning task) and provide healthier prospects for lifelong psychological adjustment by teaching children to read and work with others cooperatively in a positive group setting. My emphasis on self-efficacy has both an academic and a psychological benefit. Rebuilding self-efficacy is the primary tool that I use to foster both academic and psychological change. Vowel clustering, step-by-step reading progress, and working in a cohesive, interactive group setting are my primary tools for rebuilding self-efficacy.

Psychological and development problems. You want to emphasize the unique perspective each student brings to your program and keep your program individualized. I pretest all students so that I know what their individual needs are. I use follow-up testing to make sure that each student is progressing to the best of their ability. If I have a student who is not progressing, I work individually with the student to reevaluate and meet the student's needs. In my program, I mostly work with students experiencing academic failure. Such failure may come from a variety of problems, but I find that if I can erase academic failure in the classroom at school, I can help the student. Academic success enables students to often work through other problems. Therefore, my concentration is on erasing academic failure and rebuilding self-efficacy. An example comes from a student who failed in reading for nine straight years, had a long, long list of behavior problems at school, and lived in a very dysfunctional family and neighborhood setting. Although I could not change the family and neighborhood setting, teaching the student to read erased the behavior problems.

Developing counseling interventions. I use themes. I use 12-session subject themes (outer space exploration, ocean, environment, rainforest); alongside of these subject themes, I include counseling themes (friendship, managing anger, responsibility, consequences). Therefore, each of my learning center workstations includes both a subject theme and a counseling theme. This is illustrated in the learning center examples that I have placed at the end of each chapter in this book.

Bringing about change in mental wellness. Motivation to change is a very important component of your after-school program. I emphasize rebuilding self-efficacy. I stress hands-on learning and learning center workstations. You do not want to move your students from learning center to learning center as a small group. Moving as a group stifles individual learning. The student is either bored waiting for others to finish or unable to finish in time and thereby frustrated and embarrassed because of their inability to keep up with the group. My students move individually. They move from station to station, taking the amount of time they need at each station to complete the task. In designing my program, I include optional challenge steps for those who are able to do more. I also have the reading corner for those who may finish before others. I also try to keep my required tasks at a level everyone can complete. In this way I reduce frustration and embarrassment and increase motivation and excitement to learn.

Incorporating the 11 therapeutic factors. It is important that you build each of these therapeutic factors into your program design.

1. *Hope.* As the students see themselves improving in reading, they become excited and motivated to work even harder. They have hope. Prevention programs which teach children and teens to read have been shown through research to actually reduce the risk of depression and other risky behaviors (Kellam et al. 1994; Meyler et al. 2008). Therefore, teaching skills can help bring about hope and mental wellness.

2. *Universality.* In My *Reading Orienteering Club*, I emphasize teamwork, no bullying, never laughing or making fun of someone else, and that we are all working together to learn. My emphasis on the term *capturing tricky words* takes some of the stigma away from failure or not being able to read. As we say in my program, "It's the words that are tricky, and it's the vowel sounds that keep changing how the word is pronounced. So, let's capture those tricky words and learn all about them." Yes, the children know they missed the word, but they enjoy having some of the sting of failure taken away. Since everyone is working on tricky words, the embarrassment of not knowing a word is removed. One assignment has the children intentionally look for 100 tricky words to capture. The children read through books until they have captured 100 words. Learning becomes a game. A supportive, positive interactive group really can be a key factor in the success of your after-school program.

3. *Imparting information.* My after-school program uses learning center workstations. Learning centers and the ability to move between learning centers allow children to learn at their own pace and reduce stress and anxiety. My learning centers use hands-on, intrinsically motivating projects that serve as teaching tools. Every single craft project used in my program is a teaching tool and is used to teach about reading and working together cooperatively.

4. *Altruism.* Giving is a unique positive feature within group process. Encourage your group members to give and share support and kindness in your group, and encourage your group members to reach out and share with others outside of your group program. Giving is contagious. My children do at least three or four service projects a year. I totally believe in the benefits of service and giving to others.

5. *Peer group.* As I frequently tell my students, "I do not care how you act at home or at school; we do not act that way here at the *Reading Orienteering Club*.

We never tease, or make fun of, or hurt someone else's feelings. We are a team, and we work together to help each other." I make it clear from the very first day that I have certain expectations concerning their behavior and treatment of others in the group. Naturally, I hope that these new behaviors will transfer back to the classroom and to the neighborhood, but I must first make it clear that rude behaviors from other settings are not acceptable in my after-school program. You, not the students or the schools, set the rules for your after-school program.

6. *Social skills.* A group structure really can provide students with new ways for handling old problems. A very shy student who did not interact with other children joined my program. Instead of forcing him to work with others, I allowed him the freedom to move from station to station on his own. After a few sessions, he began to sit with others. Then, he began to talk to others. At the end of the year, he actually organized a game, invited others, and instructed others in how to play his game.

7. *Modeling.* At my program, the children have a hands-on project that they work on at each session. This may be a puppet that they will use in a puppet play or it may be a rocket covered in tricky words. The hands-on projects that the children make are always intricately connected to the learning that is taking place at the workstation. Working on projects together as a group is also motivating. A child who struggles to read may not want to work on vowel sounds, but as they see others in the group making a rocket, the reluctant child becomes more motivated to work and therefore begins to model the more cooperative behavior (Morgan et al. 2008) of those who are working. For example, a child entered my program from an alternative disciplinary school. This child was in trouble at school for fighting, on the bus, and as might be expected, started my program with the same troubled behavior. The student is now one of my top TV reporters on the weekly pretend TV show and does extra reading and research work to make sure that the TV show is ready on time. This student almost never has a behavior problem. Your after-school group becomes a real-world learning laboratory where children can learn proper behavior and group skills, but you must design these skills into your program. They will not happen automatically.

8. *Interpersonal learning.* With learning centers and the freedom to move from station to station, the children are constantly interacting in small groups at a workstation, in teams to put on a puppet play, or as problem solvers to complete a project or follow step-by-step instructions to assemble a project. Children learn to help each other and to trust one another as they interact together.

9. *Group cohesiveness.* An after-school program can become a safe place to learn and develop positive perceptions. Children are bombarded with negativism at school, from social networking through the Internet, neighborhoods, and sometimes even at home. Children need a safe place to belong, to be included. Make sure that your after-school program is completely and totally accepting of every single member, even if that member has special needs or may act a little differently than others. Acceptance is essential if you want to help improve mental well-being. Discrimination for any reason, rejection, or bullying destroys

cohesion. If your after-school program is to be cohesive, your group members and staff must demonstrate complete and total acceptance of every single participant. This does not mean that you do not have discipline. My program has rules, and rules are followed. If not, there are consequences. Cohesion means that regardless of behavior or actions, every child is accepted by the group. In my program, we say that "the behavior is unacceptable," not that a child is bad. We emphasize that we can like and accept the child without liking or accepting their behavior. Therefore, it is not the child who needs to change but the behavior.

10. *Catharsis.* No one likes to be teased, laughed at, bullied, or made fun of. Academic failure often puts students in a negative frame of reference. Failure is devastating for a young child and is compounded with embarrassment and frustration every year that failure continues. Students who are frustrated often strike out at others. Therefore, the combination of working on improving academic skills alongside improvement of social skills and group functioning enables students to feel and exhibit this sense of freedom or catharsis without inflicting harm or pain on others.

11. *Responsibility.* One lesson that children quickly learn in my program is that half-finished projects do not go home. For example, take the paper rocket that we talked about earlier. All of the children thoroughly enjoy making a rocket. They are eager to add streamers and fly the rocket around the room. To make a rocket, the child must go to all eight workstations and complete the work at all eight stations in order to have the necessary pieces to make a rocket. Our rockets are peaceful (no weapons) and only explore outer space; they are also fueled by tricky words; therefore, each child must capture enough tricky words to launch their rocket. If the child does not complete all eight stations, the rocket does not go home. As I explain, "the astronauts were not able to go into outer space in a partially completed rocket; therefore, you will need to finish your rocket before we can launch it and let you take it home." The child must return at the next session and finish the work needed to assemble and launch their rocket. This became a major point of victory with one student in my program. He could read at grade level, actually above his grade level. His comprehension was also fine. He could spell; he could write. His problem was that he absolutely never finished anything that he started. He didn't finish his homework, his tests, or reading assignments; hence, he was failing. By getting him interested in working on hands-on projects, he eventually began to see the value in completing what he started. Children soon learn that it is their responsibility to complete their work and to make sure that they stop at every single workstation. If they skip a station, the consequences of their actions quickly catch up with them.

When you write your learning center workstations, make sure that you write projects in which the children must travel to every single workstation to complete the project. Also, incorporate the academic and counseling skills that you are teaching into the project.

Real-World Applications

Observational Extensions

If possible, sit in as an observer during a group counseling session with either children or teens (or the age group for which you are designing a program). Observe how the counselor works with the group. Does the counselor incorporate group interaction? Does the counselor help the group become more cohesive? Can you see the 11 therapeutic factors at work in the group?

Troubleshooting Checklists for Organizing a New After-School Program

1. Make sure that you have both academic and counseling strategies incorporated into each and every learning center workstation.
2. Will you use themes? If so, how will you incorporate the academic and counseling themes together?
3. Does your program emphasize each of the 11 therapeutic factors?
4. Do you avoid competitive situations and encourage cooperation?
5. Is your group program interactive?
6. Do you emphasize positive group cohesion?
7. How do you emphasize acceptance?

A Ready-to-Use Group-Centered Learning Center Intervention, Designing a Learning Center to Meet the Mental Health Needs of Your Participants: Discovering the Meaning of the Word New

It is one thing to tell students that they should be kind and not tease others; it is totally different to actually design a group experience or a learning center workstation which will help students practice this principle. This is our purpose in this example. We want to teach students how to be kind and work with others in a learning environment. This is advantageous for any after-school program and will hopefully transfer back to the school classroom as well. This example illustrates how to implement the 11 therapeutic factors. Everyone wants to be included and to be liked; it is a basic psychological need (establishing hope); therefore, when we develop interventions which help the after-school group develop stronger friendship bonds, we are also developing a stronger and more cohesive peer group for our program. By establishing team partners and guiding those team partners in working together cooperatively, we reduce the fear of rejection and failure (creating universality or acceptance). By incorporating the information that we wish to teach into the learning center step-by-step instructions (imparting information), we can teach group skills and reading skills at the same workstation. By designing a situation where the students work together and act kindly toward each other, we do more than just impart information; we also strengthen counseling opportunities (to build cohesion, social skills, altruism, and modeling). By using learning center workstations with volunteer helpers at each workstation, we ensure that these counseling opportunities remain positive. If we merely turn students loose to work together, we cannot guarantee that they will actually implement the 11 therapeutic principles being taught; this is one of the benefits of using a group-centered approach (interpersonal learning). The group becomes a learning laboratory. Each learning center becomes a step in the learning process. It is the goal of a group-centered intervention, as described in this example, to teach control, acceptance, and understanding (catharsis/strong cohesive bond and responsibility). We are not only imparting information and telling students how they should act in a group setting; we are structuring interventions which encourage students to act in accordance with the principles being taught. At the same time, we are working on reading, writing, and spelling skills. This type of learning center intervention helps you develop a stronger, more cohesive after-school program.

Discovering the Meaning of the Word New

Step 1: Have you ever thought about the word *new*? Each morning starts a new day. There is also a new week, a new month, and a new year. We make new friends and have new adventures. We read a new book and capture new words. All around us, there are new things happening. Each day when we come to our after-school program, there are always new workstations waiting. The workstations are never the same; they are always new. That is why you must make sure that you go to each and every workstation. Each new day also gives us the opportunity to start over, try again, or correct some mistake that we made. For example, if I said something to hurt your feelings yesterday, I can say that I'm sorry and then work to show you that I'm telling the truth by trying to be a better friend and act kindly toward you. It isn't enough just to say that I'm sorry; I have to show you by my actions that I actually mean what I say.

Step 2: We are going to practice new things today. Find someone that you have never worked with and asked them to be your partner today. I want the two of you to go around to all of the workstations together and work as a team. Remember that when we work together as a team, we never say or do anything to hurt someone else's feelings. We want everyone to be included and feel happy.

Step 3: Your first task with your new team partner is for each of you to *capture* a new word. Remember that capturing means to find a new word that you do not know. Start at Step 1; look for a new book that you have never read before. Take turns reading out loud to your partner until you *capture* a new word. If you cannot find a word to *capture* at Step 1, then step up to Step 2. If you still cannot find a word to capture, try Step 3. Remember to take turns and work together. We never make fun or laugh at anyone. We know what it feels like to be teased or laughed at; therefore, we never tease or laugh at others. We are a team. We work together and help each other.

Step 4: Once you have each found a book and captured a new word, place a bookmark in your book. Then, write your captured word on the paper provided. Use the *4-steps* to learn your new words: say the word, spell the word and write it down correctly, give a definition for the word, and use the word in a sentence.

Step 5: Take your captured word and write a story using the word that you captured. For example, if I captured the word friendship from my book at Step 2. Then, I could write about two people who met and became friends. A story needs a beginning, middle, and ending. A story can be as short as three sentences or as long as an entire page. You decide.

Step 6: Now, I want you and your partner to blend your stories together. Take turns and read your story to your partner. How can you blend your two stories together and make one new story? For example, if my story was about friendship, and my partner's story was about travel, we could blend our two ideas together and write a story about two people who meet on a trip and become friends. The idea is to work together as a team. Have fun.

ARE YOU READY FOR A CHALLENGE?

Challenge Step: Work together and turn your story into a puppet play. Remember that when we write puppet plays, we write dialogue (or what people say) for our characters.

Chapter 4
The Role of Motivation in an Ongoing Year-Long Program

When the student started at the Reading Orienteering Club, he was very embarrassed that he could not read. He knew that he was older than most of the other children. His first defense was to pretend that he had some form of illness. He had a headache, his arm hurt, he felt dizzy, he was sick to his stomach, his eyes hurt, he could not read the words because the print was too small .... Every single day, he had a new illness. This went on for a couple of months. Through vowel clustering, I was finally able to demonstrate to him that he could actually read a story. One of the first stories that the children read at the Reading Orienteering Club is "The Story of At." It's a silly story that uses only the short vowel sound for A, as in the word AT. I complimented him after he finished reading the story the first time. It's an easy story. I use it as a motivator for beginning readers. His response was, "but I can't read." "You just did," I replied. "See, you actually read the story." "I did, didn't I," he said somewhat surprised. "Come on," I said, "I'll help you; let's read it again." It didn't happen overnight, but from that point forward, the illnesses diminished and his efforts increased. Today, he moves from learning center to learning center working at his own pace. He has multiple learning disabilities and still struggles, but he hasn't given up. The other day, while he was reading a beginning-level vowel-reader chapter book, I was worried about overtaxing his willingness to work and suggested that we stop and save the last chapter for the next session. He responded, "No, I want to finish. It's only a few more pages." I was pleased and proud to listen to him read the rest of the story.

Motivation is essential in a year-long program. Without positive, constructive intrinsic (internal) motivation, your after-school program can never succeed. Motivation is also an indispensable part of learning and mental wellness. If a student is not motivated, they will not show a desire or be willing to try. Without motivation, the student may give up or perceive that they are a failure. Such negative perceptions can lead to a state of learned helplessness or even depression (Seligman 1990).

E. Clanton Harpine, *After-School Prevention Programs for At-Risk Students: Promoting Engagement and Academic Success*, DOI 10.1007/978-1-4614-7416-6_4, © Springer Science+Business Media New York 2013

Self-efficacy is the motivational force which empowers students to succeed academically (Bandura 1977; Deci et al. 1996). Learning new skills, or learning something the student was unable to learn previously, is intrinsically motivating and exciting. Success is very encouraging. Group process, interaction, and positive group cohesion are the motivational forces which empower children and teens to achieve mental wellness. Working together with others in a supportive, cohesive group can be very satisfying—a true motivator. A group-centered after-school prevention program can serve as a working laboratory where students can experiment and develop new behaviors or approaches to learning. The question is how do you develop an after-school program which incorporates academic learning, counseling strategies to enhance well-being, and intrinsic motivation? In order to answer this question, we need to know a little bit more about motivation.

What Is Motivation?

As an after-school director or worker, the first concept that you must understand and accept is that you cannot motivate your students. Motivation comes from within. It is internal; motivation is the internal driving force that explains why students do what they do (Reeve et al. 2003). Motivation can be positive or negative and is derived from the student's experiences, perceptions of self and others, and the student's environment. The student's internal needs generate motivation— the need to be accepted, the need to be successful, and the need or desire to learn. Yes, children really do want to learn; it's an internal desire that we are all born with (Sternberg 2005). Unfortunately, negative classroom experiences, frustration, failure, and negative environmental influences can destroy this natural born desire to explore and discover new information (Katz and Assor 2007; Rogers 1969). Motivation or motivational group experiences will only be successful if they fulfill these normal intrinsic curiosities and desires to learn (Ryan and Deci 2000). These internal needs generate motivation within the student. You cannot motivate your students, but you can create motivational environments or group experiences in your after-school program which generate intrinsic (internal) motivation within the students.

All students bring three basic needs to your after-school program: (1) the need to have skills and be competent, (2) autonomy or the feeling of control, and (3) the need to be able to demonstrate the performance of specific skills successfully (Deci and Ryan 1985). When these needs are fulfilled, intrinsic motivation is generated (Urdan and Turner 2005). Such internal or intrinsic motivation occurs when students in your after-school program match an internal need or desire with the skill-building tasks being offered through your program. Every learning center must contain intrinsically motivating experiences because intrinsic motivation leads to self-determination and engaged learning (Reeve et al. 2007). Therefore, you must build intrinsic motivators into your after-school program.

What Is the Difference Between Intrinsic and Extrinsic Motivation?

Most public schools and many after-school community programs use food, monetary awards, prizes, or other extrinsic rewards to motivate children to participate and complete learning assignments. When after-school programs rely on prizes and rewards for compliance (stickers, candy, cookies, or even pizza), such after-school programs may actually dampen a student's intrinsic desire to learn (Lepper and Greene 1975; Reeve et al. 2007). Students work only when rewarded, and tend to look for easier routes for securing the expected award, such as reading beginning-level books to receive quicker rewards rather than taking on a challenging chapter book (Thorkildsen 2002). As a third-grade student explained: "We have to keep a reading log and tell our teacher how many books we read at home. I read little baby books; they're fast and easy. As soon as I read ten books, I get to pick a prize out of the basket."

Relying on prizes may also motivate students to work just hard enough to get the desired prize and then totally quit and not continue to pursue learning opportunities (such as reading other books or harder books), unless promised another prize (Fawson and Moore 1999). This point was exemplified by a young first grader in my after-school *Reading Orienteering Club* program. The young man was constantly in trouble. Even as he arrived each day, the community worker who delivered him after school to my program was constantly taking him aside to talk about his behavior. During our section on outer space exploration, he became very excited about building a paper rocket. As is customary in my program, in order to build his rocket, he had to travel around to all eight workstations. Each workstation stressed vowel clustering, reading stories, and capturing tricky words (words they did know). The children were to *capture tricky words* as they traveled to each workstation and then use these captured words in making and decorating their rocket. The little boy was not interested in doing any work; he just wanted to make a rocket. He threw a fit the first day when told that he could not take a partially finished rocket home. He was told that he could work on his rocket again at the next session. At the next session, he behaved, worked hard, and finished his rocket. As soon as his rocket was finished, he started running around the room and misbehaving again. The rocket was placed up on a high shelf where it stayed for several weeks. As expected, the little boy continually demanded his rocket. He was told, "we have work to do today; we'll talk about the rocket later." Even on days when he behaved, the rocket was not returned. He was only given the rocket to take home after he completely stopped asking about the rocket and worked cooperatively for several weeks. I did not want the rocket to become a reward for good behavior; therefore, I did not give him the rocket as expected on the days that he behaved. Although just a first grader, this student had previously learned the extrinsic-reward pattern. He behaved just long enough to get what he wanted, his rocket. Then, he planned to go off and do as he pleased. I wanted to break this pattern; therefore, I did not follow his expectations. He was not rewarded for behaving; none of the children in my program are extrinsically rewarded for good behavior.

Six weeks later, the assignment was to make a pop-up book about traveling to the moon. The same little boy finished his pop-up rocket decorated with tricky words (vowel clustering) and his pop-up moon on which he wrote facts that he had learned (comprehension) about the moon. Once his book was assembled, it was discovered that he had skipped a workstation. Getting to this point was a major accomplishment for the student, but instead of being allowed to stop, the little boy was sent back to the station that he had skipped to write a story. I encouraged him by saying, "why don't you write a story telling us what would happen if you traveled to the moon?" He returned a few minutes later with a story and a picture to go in his book. He proudly sauntered down to the TV studio to read his story.

Good behavior is an expectation of all participants. If you want to reduce a child's dependence upon extrinsic rewards (prizes), you must be consistent and make sure that the child will not perceive your actions as being a reward. That is why I waited for several weeks before allowing the rocket to go home, and then I sent the rocket home on a day when other children were taking projects home. That is also why I did not allow the student to skip writing a story for his pop-up book. The hands-on craft projects used throughout my *Reading Orienteering Club* program are teaching tools. The object is not to simply make a craft. The craft project becomes a hands-on means of teaching and motivating children to practice vowel clustering. Regardless whether the children are making a rocket, a giant fish, puppets, a pop-up book, or *Ollie Octopus*, the children must travel to all eight workstations in order to complete their project. Unfinished projects never go home. The children are given time in a later session or during free time to finish any projects that they have not had a chance to complete. To finish a project, the child must go back and complete the actual work that was assigned for that particular project; therefore, the objective is never to just make a craft. The purpose of the craft project is to teach children to follow step-by-step directions and to follow through and complete what they start. These are two very important lessons for life.

Extrinsic rewards (prizes) strip away children's intrinsic motivation to learn, and prizes or awards also reduce the quality of learning (Benware and Deci 1984). When children are motivated by rewards, they focus on producing a quick answer that will secure the reward, but they do not analyze or solve problems (Condry and Chambers 1978; Ryan and Deci 2008). When you use extrinsic rewards, children lose the joy of learning new information or solving a problem; they are simply going through the motions (Thorkildsen 2002). The negative effect of extrinsic rewards is true for both adolescents and adults as well (Deci 2009; Stone et al. 2009).

Is the After-School Group Environment Important?

The group environment upon which your after-school program is built is critical to the success or the failure of your program. Your after-school group environment will either generate intrinsic motivation or fail. Your goal is to make sure that your program stimulates and responds to the internal, intrinsic needs of your students. You want your students to become engaged, self-regulating learners (Zimmerman and Kitsantas 2005). Self-regulation is when a child regulates their own behavior and actions. Self-regulation includes a student choosing to learn rather than being assigned or forced or coerced into learning. Self-regulation also includes when a student chooses to work longer on the task than required. This includes both persistence (how long someone is willing to try) and effort (how hard someone is willing to work). Self-regulation is a necessary life-skill that children must develop in order to become successful, happy adults. Extrinsic rewards interfere with the development of self-regulation (Ryan and Deci 2000). Intrinsic motivation encourages self-regulation (Deci et al. 1981).

The importance of self-regulation and intrinsic motivation was definitely exemplified by a group at my *Reading Orienteering Club* after-school program. Four students were given the opportunity to be *On the Spot* reporters for the weekly make-believe TV show. An assortment of challenging reading material on space travel (our theme was outer space exploration) was made available to the children. They each selected a book. Much of the reading material contained words that the children did not know; therefore, they were constantly looking words up in the dictionary. Their task was to read and write a report using Who, What, When, Where, and Why. Workstation helpers helped with the difficult reading material and writing their report.

The *Reading Orienteering Club* program is a 2-hour session. The children voluntarily stayed at the TV workstation reading and writing reports for the entire 2-hours session instead of rotating to another workstation. The task was hard. They had the option to go to a different workstation to build a rocket; yet these children continued working on their task. One student brought her report to me. When I said, "that's excellent, make sure your name is on your report, then go to the next station." She replied, "I'm going to work more; I want it to be really good." Their goal was to be ready for the upcoming TV show. Every child participates in every single show; therefore, these children were not to be singled out for praise or a starring role. I use only intrinsic motivators; there are no prizes or rewards for extra effort. They were simply tackling and completing a hard task. No one gave up, no one quit, and no one in the group even considered that they could not perform the task requested. Two of the children in this group had repeatedly failed reading at school until they joined the *Reading Orienteering Club*. After being in the program for a year, these two students are now receiving passing grades in reading at school. The other two children (in their first year) had only been in the *Reading Orienteering Club* for approximately 8 weeks; yet, they too willingly accepted a challenging assignment. Remember, we mentioned earlier that each student works at their own pace; one child may be able to learn in 1 year, while another child may need 2 or possibly even 3 years to erase failure and bring their school work up to passing or above. This is the advantage of an after-school program. You can individualize instruction, motivation, and group participation. Such individualized programming doesn't happen by accident or just because you organize a group; you must build intrinsic motivation and self-regulation into your program.

Building Motivation into Your After-School Program

Hands-on activities generate motivation. Hands-on activities intrinsically motivate children and teens to interact with the learning process and with others in the group. Intrinsic activities (internal not reward based) help students develop a positive attitude towards learning and a feeling of accomplishment when they are successful in learning a new skill. Sometimes children want to give up and not finish. Intrinsically oriented hands-on activities can motivate students to tackle harder tasks, to challenge themselves to do more, and to try again instead of giving up and quitting. Pop-up books and rockets are two of the favorite activities in my reading program. As I stated previously, I have a policy that unfinished books or rockets do not go home until each step is completed. Watching another child fly their rocket around the room with streamers fluttering is very motivating, particularly if you keep repeating that you would be happy to help them finish their rocket too. No rewards, no prizes, just completion of a hands-on project—intrinsic. The same is true of pop-up books. Each book has three or four pages that pop-up. The children read, follow directions, and write stories before their book is completed. The excitement of making a book with pages that pop-up is very motivating. Therefore, as you design your after-school program, think how you will build motivation into your program. I use hands-on paper craft projects with young children. Creating a make-believe TV studio and TV show works very well with older elementary students and teenagers. All ages learn best when they're totally engaged in the learning process. Worksheets, workbooks, or taking notes from a lecture or PowerPoint presentation do not fit the intrinsic needs of students; therefore, typical classroom teaching techniques will not help you create an intrinsically motivating learning environment for your after-school program. Use hands-on learning techniques instead; engage your students in the learning process. To succeed, your program must meet the students' academic and emotional needs.

Self-efficacy is motivating. Self-efficacy (the belief that you can complete a task), unlike pure social emotional programming, is linked to the central mission of community after-school programs in that self-efficacy addresses both the academic and mental health needs of the students (Bandura 1977). Self-efficacy affects how well children apply the skills and knowledge they have attained while generating persistence and willingness to work on difficult tasks (Bandura 1997). A child's ability to read comes from the skills the child learns. Expectancy is high until the child fails (Bandura, 1997). Self-confidence is lowered every time the child fails. An after-school program can provide a supportive atmosphere within which self-efficacy can be rebuilt. Being successful is very motivating, especially if the child has failed in their past experiences. Children who are referred to my *Reading Orienteering Club* after-school program usually arrive with low self-efficacy. The first thing they tell me is that a teacher, parent, or someone has told them that they cannot read leaving them convinced that they will never be able to learn to read. When they leave my program, they are reading and very excited about reading. In the 4 years that my

Reading Orienteering Club program has been in existence, every student (who completes the year-long program) has made improvement (Clanton Harpine 2012). Students are motivated when they see themselves improving, so rebuilding self-efficacy becomes an essential component for a successful after-school program.

Success leads to motivation. Self-efficacy fulfills a major step in motivation because students are encouraged when they succeed or discouraged when they fail to learn a new task. I develop and design my after-school program to lead the students to success. *Vowel clustering* is one of the key factors to rebuild self-efficacy. Children who have never been able to read a story before can learn to read a story in the first week of the program. Refer back to the example story in Chap. 1. *The Hat Cat* story uses only the simple short *ă sound as in the word at. Once children have mastered the short ă sound, they are ready to begin reading simple stories as long as you make sure that the story uses only the one vowel sound that has been taught. Students who have never been able to read before are excited the first time they read a simple vowel-clustered story. They know that it is only a beginning, but now they hope that they may actually be able to go on and learn to read more challenging stories. Success really is motivating, so build success steps into your after-school program.*

Topics of interest or themes help to keep motivation soaring. One of the hardest aspects of a year-long after-school program is keeping motivation high throughout a 9- or a 12-month program. I use themes. My *Reading Orienteering Club* program contains 12-session theme packets. They are All about Books, Outer Space Exploration, the Ocean, Pollution and the Benefits of Recycling, Exploring a Rainforest, the Weather, A Moment in History, and Extinct Animals. Each 12-session theme packet stresses vowel clustering, reading, writing, spelling, and historical and scientific information on a particular theme. The themes generate interest and help to make sure that there is always something new and different going on at the *Reading Orienteering Club.*

Group process helps to bring motivation about. You need to create an atmosphere with your after-school program that supports motivation. My *Reading Orienteering Club* teaches remedial reading skills, phonics, sight words, writing as well as reading, spelling, comprehension, and fluency, and also helps children rebuild their self-efficacy by allowing them to work in a nonjudgmental atmosphere. Challenging activities push the children to work slightly above their present level of development, thus learning new skills and solving old problems. Play is the language of children, and children learn best through hands-on activities. The *Reading Orienteering Club* accomplishes this by using action-oriented, hands-on learning centers and one-on-one remedial assistance. The *Reading Orienteering Club* is more than simply a remedial reading program. It is a motivational efficacy retraining program set in the safe atmosphere of a therapeutic group. In this setting, children not only learn, but they also learn to feel good about themselves. How will you create an atmosphere which supports motivation in your group program?

Creating an Intrinsically Motivating After-School Program

Intrinsic motivation does not automatically occur when you organize a group; it must be created. There are six types of intrinsic motivators that you can use in your program design: positive self-efficacy, efficacy expectations, outcome expectations, choice, competence-affirming feedback, and self-determination (Ryan and Deci 2000). We will first identify each motivator; then discuss how to develop each motivator in your after-school program. The *Reading Orienteering Club* program is an example to illustrate how each motivator can be applied.

Self-efficacy. Self-efficacy is vital to the academic, counseling, and motivational goals of your program. Students need to experience improvement before they will believe that they can actually change, and they need the thrill of success in order to motivate them to seek this change. You cannot teach students if they do not believe it is possible for them to learn. Therefore, build into your program a way for students to see themselves improving. I use vowel-clustered stories so that students move up one step at a time but can succeed in the first week of the program.

Efficacy expectations (persistence and control). Effort and persistence stem from positive self-efficacy. If I do not believe that I can accomplish a task or complete a project, I will not put forth much effort. A sense of control is important if I am to be persuaded to put forth my best effort. When we say that students need to exercise control, we do not mean that students may do whatever they please. Efficacy expectations or exercising control means that the student is allowed to choose among appropriate actions. For example, students might choose a book from a stack offered at a reading step, rather than having a book assigned to them. Also, allowing variety in how a project is decorated gives students an element of control.

Outcome expectations (persistence and effort). For students to become successful in life, they must learn to put forth effort and persistence. Learning to complete a challenging project instead of giving up and quitting encourages students to learn to put forth their best effort. It helps to have some easy projects, some short-term challenging projects, and some long-term projects. Mixing up the amount of effort and persistence which must be put forward helps to motivate students. If everything is hard and seemingly impossible, then many students simply give up. If, on the other hand, some projects are easy while others are hard, the student then begins to learn that effort and persistence can make the difference.

Choice. To succeed students must be motivated. To be motivated, students must experience the desire to learn, to change their behavior, or to be successful (Deci 1971). Intrinsic motivation creates this desire (Sternberg 2005). Students need to feel the freedom to choose, so build flexibility into your program. For example, in my program, students travel around the room to eight workstations. They must go to each station in order to complete their project for the day, but they have the freedom to choose the order in which they complete the stations. This element of choice is very motivating.

Competence-affirming feedback. Everyone wants to be successful. Success is rewarding and motivating. Children get excited when they complete a project, but no two children are the same, work in the same manner, or learn through the same techniques. Although positive comments are good, praise simply for the sake of praise is not motivating. Students need to experience success, completion of a project, and pride in what they have done. *For example, in my program, students look at steps as being challenges because they are constantly finding new books at reading stations: Step 1, Step 2, and Step 3. They learn to tackle new challenges one step at a time; therefore, small accomplishments are still perceived by the students as positive learning accomplishments.*

Self-determination. Your group can become an important ingredient in creating an intrinsically motivating environment, but students must learn through the group to accept responsibility for their actions, to develop commitment, and to become self-directed. Students must learn to make the choice to want to learn, but this will not happen overnight. A strong group structure though can lead at-risk students and teach them to become responsible group participants. *It is motivating, for example, for beginning readers to be able to read a story. Unfortunately, as mentioned earlier, most beginning early reading commercial and/or school textbooks cover five or more vowel sounds in each story. This means that beginning readers must learn at least five or six vowel sounds before they can even begin to read a story. Failure is not motivating. You want to build success into your program so that your students will be able to successfully display their skills and know that they have made a true accomplishment. Learning new skills one step at a time is not discouraging, especially if you build step-by-step processes into your program.*

Step 4: Designing a Learning Center to Enhance Intrinsic Motivation

How will you make self-efficacy (motivator #1) positive and motivating?

How will you encourage persistence (motivator #2)?

How will you demonstrate improvement (motivator #3)? How will you make sure that your measures of improvement are not interpreted negatively by the students?

How will you enable the students to exercise choice (motivator #4), yet still keep control and structure in your program?

How will you challenge your students (motivator #5)? How will you make sure that your hands-on projects are not too difficult and therefore interpreted negatively by the students?

How will you help your students become self-directed (motivator #6)?

How will you ensure that your motivators are truly intrinsic and not extrinsic? How will you determine that your intrinsic motivators are truly working?

Step 4, Design Example

1. *Self-efficacy as a motivator.* As pointed out earlier, vowel clustering is one of my primary instructional tools for rebuilding self-efficacy. It is also one of my primary motivators. In my program, the children make a puppet named *Andy the Ant. Andy* is a simple project that each child can easily make. The learning center workstations have simple vowel-clustered stories using short *ă sound words about Andy. The children are encouraged to practice reading and capturing short ă sound words as they travel from learning center to learning center making legs for Andy, adding eyes, and constructing his body. On each leg, they write a list of captured* short *ă sound words to take home and practice. Learning becomes motivating. This is an easy project that is made early in the program. It is easy so that I can guarantee success for every student, and, since the project teaches only one vowel sound, there is no confusion. Older students ready for a little more challenge read the puppet play at the close of the session. The Andy the Ant puppets become ants at an anthill in the puppet play. Everyone is included. Self-efficacy teaches success and motivates.*
2. *Effort and persistence.* Effort and persistence must be built up gradually, so I have my students read chapter books during our first 12-week session. Most students groan when I mention the word chapter book or say, "the print is too small it makes my eyes hurt" or "I'll never be able to finish a chapter book." Therefore, I introduce my students to chapter books very slowly. Our first

12-week theme is called *All about Books*. At one of my workstations, we have our own small library (books which have been donated to the program). There are baskets for Step 1, Step 2, and Step 3. At each step, I place very thin beginning chapter books. Step 1 actually has vowel reading chapter books which cover only one vowel sound at a time. If I cannot find an appropriate book for all of my students, I write one. In this way, even my very beginning readers can read a chapter book. The books at Step 2 are a little bit harder. The books at Step 3 are the most challenging. I try to keep 10–20 books in each basket so that the children have several books to choose from. Each child starts at Step 1 and reads until they capture five *tricky* words. Even my best readers start at Step 1. Students move up gradually. If they do not capture five tricky words at Step 1, then they move to Step 2. If they do not capture five tricky words at Step 2, then they move up to Step 3. In this way everyone is selecting a book and reading at their ability level. At each session, they select another book to read. By the third week, students have selected a chapter book for which they will write a report and decorate a costume. Each session has comprehension questions that encourage the students to think about the main character in their chapter book. By the end of the 12-week theme, the students have painted a costume which tells something about the main character in their book. They also write a report to give on the make-believe TV show, telling about the book that they have read. There is a day set aside for making hats, glasses, or whatever else the student needs to complete their costume and show off the character from their book. Everyone is having fun while they learn and quickly forget their fear of chapter books.

3. *Measuring improvement positively*. In my program, each student has a spiral notebook. From day one, they list words that they capture (miss) in their notebook as they travel to each workstation. Midway through the program, they make a magic word box which contains 100 captured words. For 1 week, they read stories at each workstation searching for words to capture. They also search through their spiral notebook, rereading words they captured over the semester. If they still find any of these words to be tricky (words they miss), they add them to their list. Then, use the *4-step method* to learn the word. It becomes a game and the children quickly go out to see how many words they can capture. At each workstation they try to add 12 new tricky words and add a decorated side to their box. The words are added to a long list which can be pulled through the box. Each workstation offers a different way to decorate the box. By the midpoint, the children are often surprised how many words from their spiral notebook are no longer tricky for them. This simple project shows the child how much they have improved but is a lot more fun than taking a test.

4. *Choice*. It is important to allow students the freedom to make choices as they learn, but it is also very important for them to learn to work within your program's structure and rules. When making a pop-up house for their first book, each student uses the same pattern to make their house (every book has a house), but students then decorate and make windows and doors for their house to fit their own individual ideas. Instead of having every project be exactly the same, the projects then reflect the individual personalities of the students. Students may

choose the color of paper that they wish to use to make their house and then decorate their house very simply by drawing a window and a door or very elaborately by making shutters, window boxes, or even windowpanes. The choice is left to the student. The project is simple enough for every student to complete, but also motivates students to do more than what is required. To finish their book, students must follow the rules and go to each workstation, working the reading and writing assignments at each station. For example, every pop-up book contains an original story written by the student. Each story must be edited for grammar and spelling before it may be placed in the pop-up book. Children then rewrite their edited stories, using their best handwriting. Pop-up books do not go home until the story is in its final edited version. Again, the objective is not just to make a pop-up house. The objective is to teach children to write grammatical sentences with words which are spelled correctly. The pop-up house activity also adds reading and following step-by-step directions which increases comprehension. The fun of making a pop-up house book makes children want to tackle a harder task.

5. *Challenge, persistence, and effort.* In my program, when the children study the vowel sound for AL, they make *Allie the Alligator.* Allie is made from recycled materials and also includes some challenging steps. Everyone can make the basic alligator, but they must choose whether they wish to add teeth to the alligator. Yes, the teeth are a bit more challenging to make and glue into the alligator's mouth. As always, the alligator can only be completed by working at each of the eight workstations and completing the vowel or reading assignments at each station. Allie is a tool which encourages students to want to learn. I can't motivate the students, but I can provide projects which help generate motivation within the students.

6. *Being self-directed.* To become self-directed, students must choose to apply skills, exert more effort, and work beyond the minimum requirements of an assignment. One of the last projects that my students work on at the end of the year is to choose an animal to learn about. They read nonfiction stories and research information in order to write a report about their animal. The report may be two sentences or several pages long. They type the report on the computer and then make a pop-up book about their animal. They also write a make-believe fictional story about their animal. They then give an oral report for their make-believe TV show and participate in a puppet play at the closing program. This project takes several weeks, and there are minimum requirements at each workstation. Yet, the students always exceed those minimum requirements, putting more effort and work into their final project than is required.

I keep my motivators intrinsic by making sure that they are never perceived as rewards. Every single student makes every project. Some projects allow students to choose to add more complicated or difficult details, but there is always a basic project that every single student can complete. I conduct periodic follow-up testing to make sure that my students are progressing with their reading skills. If my students are not learning, then my motivators are not successful. The goal is to teach children to read in order to give them a chance to live a happier and more successful life. Intrinsic motivators and hands-on projects are used to help achieve that goal.

Real-World Applications

Observational Extensions

Observe an after-school program. How motivated do the students seem to be? How can you tell that they are motivated? What could you do to make this program more successful and increase the motivation of the students participating?

Troubleshooting Checklists for Organizing a New After-School Program

1. Check your after-school program design. Are you using intrinsic or extrinsic motivators? How can you get rid of any extrinsic motivators?
2. Are you using punishments, reprimands, or extrinsic incentives in your program? If so, how can you change these to be more intrinsic?
3. Is your after-school program motivating? What will you do if your students do not find your program to be motivating?

A Ready-to-Use Group-Centered Learning Center Intervention, Designing a Learning Center to Meet the Intrinsic Motivational Needs of Your Participants: Matt the Rat

This example illustrates how to apply the six types of motivation. The motivational power of *self-efficacy* is demonstrated through using a simple vowel-clustered story that all children will be able to read. There are seven different vowel combinations which combine together to make the *long ā vowel sound*. By presenting only two of those vowel sounds (silent E and AI) at a time, this provides *challenge* but also ensures that children will be able to learn and advance in their quest to learn the vowel clusters. Incorporating an easy step-by-step hands-on craft project encourages children to read and follow directions and teaches that by applying *effort and persistence* children can learn to follow directions and complete simple projects. The craft project also allows children to exhibit a degree of *choice* in how they decorate the rat and offers a *challenge* when children are asked to write an ending to the story. This might be a simple one-sentence ending, or the student may decide to write a long detailed ending for the story. The student *controls* how much effort they feel comfortable putting into their story. An additional challenge and avenue for self-direction are offered in the form of a puppet play. Children not only write but also work with others' plan and present their puppet play. This type of activity could be expanded across any number of workstations. For the craft in this example, you may make circle patterns for the children to trace or simply set out three different size containers and allow the children to trace around the containers to make their circles. This example is also written with workstation helpers in mind so that the children who need help would have help readily accessible.

MATT THE RAT

Step 1: For the past few sessions, we have been studying vowel sounds for the letter A. you will remember that we talked about the short ă *sound as in the word at. We said that when a word had only one syllable (one complete sound) and one vowel, such as with A, then that word most likely would use* the short ă *sound. Read the following list of words and use the* short ă *sound. If you capture any tricky words, make sure that you write them down. Read the following:* cat, hat, fan, sand, cab, had, back, black.

Step 2: We have also been learning that when there are two vowels in a syllable, one may be silent but make the first vowel use its letter name, such as with the word *ate*. The E is silent and the A uses the *long ā vowel sound*. AI can make A say its name as well. The I is silent and the letter A uses the *long ā vowel sound*, straight. Read the following story. Watch carefully for silent E and AI. Write down any tricky words that you capture because we will be using these captured words in just a few minutes.

Matt the Rat

Matt the Rat takes the bait from the trap.

Matt makes a cake with the bait.

Matt takes the cake to the lake.

Step 3: You're the author. What do you think Matt will do at the lake? Write at least one sentence telling what you think will happen next in this story. You may also write several pages telling about Matt's adventure. You're the author; you decide. Have your workstation helper edit your story. Then write a final copy. Would you like to read your story for our TV show at the end of our session today? We'd love to hear your story.

Step 4: Now it's time to have some fun with Matt the Rat. Trace four circles—one large, one medium, and two small circles. Use the containers provided on the table to help you make circles. On the back of your largest circle, write your name at the top and then write each of the words that you captured in Step 1 (short *ă sound words*). Now write each of the words that you captured in Step 2. For each word that you captured, use the *4-step method* and practice the captured word: say the word, spell and use the word in a sentence, give a definition of the word, and write the word correctly on the back of your largest circle. If you did not capture any words in Step 1 and Step 2, then write three short *ă sound words and four long ā vowel sound words, two using silent E and two using AI. Place these on the back of your largest circle.*

Step 5: Next, use the middle-sized circle. There is a tricky word that has the letter A and silent E but does not use the *long ā vowel sound.* Do you know which word it is? If you're not sure and need a hint, reread the directions for Step 2. Our tricky word is hiding in the first sentence. Write this tricky word on the back of your middle circle.

Step 6: We are now ready to put our puppet together. Follow the directions carefully. You are going to make a Matt the Rat puppet. The largest circle is the body, the middle-sized circle is the head, and the two smallest circles are the ears. Glue the edge of the head to the top edge of the body. Draw a nose and eyes or use scraps of paper to make a nose and eyes. Be creative. Make a fancy puppet. Glue ears in place on the head. You may even add whiskers for your rat by cutting tiny slithers of scrap paper and gluing them in place. Set aside to dry while you make the tail.

Step 7: Your rat's tail may be as long as you wish as long as it is covered with tricky words. Cut a long slither of paper, just large enough for you to write on. If you have trouble writing on a thin slither of paper, write first and then cut your paper. Your words will be in one long string. Write as many tricky short *ă sound* words and long *ā sound* words (using *silent E* and *AI*) as possible. Try to think of at least ten words. You may even use words from this page. Short *ă* and *silent E* are easy, but if you have trouble thinking of *AI*, here's a hint—*fail, tail, pail, mail, sail.* And yes, you may use the dictionary if you need help. Once you have finished, glue the tail in place on the large circle. Take a pencil and curl the tail. Glue the large circle to a stick or a stiff piece of cardboard to use as the handle for your puppet. Your rat puppet is complete.

ARE YOU READY FOR A CHALLENGE?

Challenge Step: Write a puppet play for Matt the Rat. Remember that when we write a puppet play, we write for the characters and write down what each character would say. Have Matt meet two friends at the lake. What would Matt and his friends do? Once you finish writing, have your workstation helper edit your work. Then, find two group members to help you with your puppet play. Practice reading and be ready for today's TV show.

Chapter 5
Group Process, Self-Efficacy, and Cohesion: Applying the Principles of Change

He was a third grader when he joined my Reading Orienteering Club program. He was one of four siblings, and the only child in the family who could not read. He had been diagnosed by the public schools as having dyslexia. He was so frustrated that he refused to even try. He informed me on the first day, "You know I have dyslexia and can't read." I smiled and said, "I'll help you learn to read, and I promise that you're going to love it when you learn to read. Reading is so exciting and so much fun." This dialogue continued for the first few sessions. He explained each time that he had dyslexia and could not read, but gradually through vowel clustering he began to see himself slowly reading. He would start to say, "You know I . . . ." I would always break in and respond, "I know isn't it exciting to read; wait until you see what we are reading today." After about 2 months in the program, he mastered his word reversal problems, reading from left to right instead of right to left, and began to see how words were composed of sounds. Instead of guessing, he sounded out the letters and tried to read everything that crossed his path. By the end of the year, he was reading beginning-level chapter books. He didn't need the program a second year; he returned to school excited to read. The year after, I checked with his parents just to make sure how he was doing. He had moved up two grade levels in reading. He was still struggling a bit with sentence construction, but I smiled when his father said, "You can't keep a book out of his hands. Everywhere he goes he takes a book to read."

The purpose of every after-school program should be to bring about positive, constructive change (Granger et al. 2007). The change might be to help students learn new ways of acting (behavior) and new academic skills, or to develop new techniques for interacting with others in a group setting. You decide what kind of change you want to bring about in your after-school program. Group-centered after-school prevention programs, such as my *Reading Orienteering Club*, integrate learning and counseling, make full use of group process by stressing interaction and cohesion, stress intrinsic (internal) motivation rather than extrinsic (rewards or prizes), and

E. Clanton Harpine, *After-School Prevention Programs for At-Risk Students: Promoting Engagement and Academic Success*, DOI 10.1007/978-1-4614-7416-6_5, © Springer Science+Business Media New York 2013

seek to rebuild self-efficacy (belief that the student can accomplish a task) by giving emphasis to *vowel clustering*.

Children from at-risk environments need programs that emphasize step-by-step procedures and active hands-on learning to bring about change (Jensen et al. 2007; Trout et al. 2007). They also need a constructive supportive group. The student described above had been in one-on-one tutoring since kindergarten, but he could not read, nor was he optimistic when he joined my group. Failure was very deeply ingrained, and he saw failure as the only outcome. Yet, when he saw others struggling in the group and started learning *vowel clustering* skills which did in fact help him begin to learn to read, he began to think that there just might possibly be hope. At first, he was still doubtful, but then step by step, he began to read harder and harder books, until he too was convinced that he really could read. Without the group structure, he might never have taken the chance to try again.

The Role of the Group in Bringing About Change

Groups help students increase their self-awareness; a deeper understanding of self can lead to a greater willingness to try and change. Many researchers point out that it is easier for students to change while participating in a group (Brigman and Webb 2007). Groups provide interaction which helps participants acquire skills (Buhs et al. 2006). It is also easier for students to change their attitudes or ways of behaving while participating in a group (Horne et al. 2007). Groups create their own culture, which helps students develop a sense of belonging. Groups provide feedback and help students feel included. This is particularly important for at-risk students. Research shows that positive, supportive groups can help at-risk students change their behavior (Kulic et al. 2004), but not all groups are helpful. As mentioned earlier, this is particularly true with after-school groups (Granger 2010). A positive group experience depends on how group process develops during group sessions.

Group Dynamics and Group Process

There are two forces at work in every group: group dynamics and group process. Group dynamics refers to the individual members of your group and the personalities and communication styles that each person brings to the group. As we discussed earlier every single student in your after-school program is an individual. They have individual learning needs, ideas and feelings, personalities, perceptions, fears, and individual ways of behaving in a group setting. No two members of your group are the same, not even identical twins. Therefore, you must look at each member of your group as a unique and distinct individual. You cannot group your students together and say that "I work with a group of students who have been diagnosed with ADHD" or "I work with at-risk teenagers." No two groups are alike, and no two students in a group are alike. The dynamics of your group will determine how the students in your program respond to the changes that you propose, so you must be prepared for multiple reactions to the group interventions and techniques that you use in your after-school program.

Group process refers to what happens in your group. Group process includes the interaction between group members and the interventions and group techniques that you use in your group to bring about change. Skill-building activities to rebuild self-efficacy, intrinsic motivators to generate self-direction, and structured interactive exercises to create cohesion are all part of group process and how you use group process to bring about change. Throughout this book we have been discussing how to structure and develop group process within your after-school program so that it will lead to positive outcomes and the change that you seek with your group of students. Cohesion is the key to change in groups (Marmarosh et al. 2005). Cohesion develops first as support and acceptance (Holtz 2004). It then grows into learning and development (Yalom and Leszcz 2005). In order to have cohesion in your after-school program, you must have interaction (Clanton Harpine 2013a, b). You cannot simply sit students down in a circle of chairs and lecture to them; that is not group interaction. Nor can you just sit and talk. In order to bring about change, your group interaction must be constructive interaction. After-school groups that gather just for recreational activities do not bring forth the kind of group interaction that is needed for personal growth, development, and change (Roth et al. 2010). Competition is not cohesive; therefore, any time you permit competition in your after-school program, you have turned the group away from cohesion. You cannot have both cohesion and competition; they do not mix.

Group Process Encourages Change

For group process to be effective the group must include interaction and cohesion (Ablon and Jones 2002) and there must be a desire, willingness, or motivation to change. At-risk students need the strength of a cohesive group in order to make changes in their behavior and interactions with others (Deci et al. 1996). Therefore, it becomes essential that you build interaction and cohesion into your after-school program. Gathering students together in a group and simply allowing them to talk is not the type of interaction that we are striving for. For an after-school program to be effective in bringing about change, we need to structure group interaction. Rebuilding self-efficacy is one of the most important steps for change in education. Cohesion is the key to change in group therapy (Yalom and Leszcz 2005). Interaction is strategic to success in group prevention (Conyne 2004). When we combine these factors with group process, we pull together the strongest possible elements of change, and this is what we need in after-school programming.

Prevention Programs Lead to Change

Prevention-focused activities create healthy well-being and a climate of change (Weissberg et al. 2003), but be careful, as stated earlier, many after-school programs are tacking on the prevention label without following the principles of group prevention. If you are truly running an after-school prevention program, your group program must use positive, constructive group interaction, which leads to cohesion (Conyne and Clanton Harpine 2010). Cohesion is only possible when every member of your group feels accepted and comfortable interacting with every other member of the group—no one is ostracized, no one is teased, and no one is laughed at or made fun of. Cohesion is not easy to achieve, but it must always be your primary goal.

Cohesion Guides Change

Interaction in a positive group setting encourages acceptance and decision-making by group members. Such acceptance leads to cohesion. Cohesion reinforces the sense of belonging, trust, and positive acceptance that is so essential for constructive change (Yalom and Leszcz 2005). Group interventions can be used to bring about this constructive change (Finn et al. 2005), but if the group is to become a positive pathway to change, the group intervention must include constructive educationally oriented skill-building (Toppelberg et al. 2006). An effective after-school program must also provide organizational skills. Problem-solving skills, steps for dealing with frustration, and awareness to foresee the consequences of one's actions are also essential elements of an effective after-school program.

In my own after-school program, I use painting a puppet stage as a problem-solving group activity to increase interaction and cohesion. The children work in small groups to first design what they would like to paint. Each small group then combines their ideas with others to create a final group design. Everyone must agree upon the final details of the design; no ideas may be rejected. The students then work together to paint what they have designed. The problem is that they have one puppet stage to paint and 30 students. They must compromise and work together to develop a design that incorporates everyone's ideas—no one can be left out. Then they must work together to give everyone a chance to paint. At-risk students need to learn ways to control impulsivity and deal with distractions. Painting a simple puppet stage becomes a wonderful way to teach problem-solving and decision-making. Interpersonal group skills are important life skills. If at-risk students are to learn ways to change behavioral problems and incorporate new approaches to learning, they must interact with others in a positive, cohesive group setting. Working together with others on a common project can sometimes be one of the best means of bringing about this interactive change.

Group-Centered Creative Art Interventions

Group-centered creative art interventions can be used to bring about change with at-risk students because they create constructive interaction within the group. A creative art intervention is typically hands-on. With children group-centered interventions usually involve some kind of craft project or play acting. Creative art interventions may involve either individual or group projects as long as they work to strengthen efforts to rebuild self-efficacy and psychological wellness. Creative art group-centered interventions can help at-risk children change unwanted, disruptive classroom behaviors and foster psychological development and well-being as well as academic success. Creative art interventions have a healing, therapeutic quality (Malchiodi 2007). The creative process works as an agent of change (Malchiodi 2011). When combined with the therapeutic structure of group process, group-centered creative art interventions can be used to help children relax, focus, and learn new group behavior (Lusebrink 2010). Creative Art Therapy has a long-standing history as a therapeutic intervention (Rubin 2005).

For example, the *Reading Orienteering Club* features weekly and monthly craft-oriented group-centered creative art intrinsic interventions. During the *Ocean* theme, children paint a coral reef puppet stage to use with their giant paper fish puppets. A painting intervention teaches teamwork and research skills. The children work in teams to read and learn about the coral reef. Then, they create with paint and other craft supplies a representation of what they've read about. For example, to create the various layers and textures of the coral reef, the children add sand, coffee, ground pepper seasoning, pebbles, dyed cotton stuffing, and even twists of tissue paper. They read, research, and look at pictures to recreate their representation of a coral reef. This creative art intervention pulls learning and counseling objectives together in one project. Self-efficacy is emphasized because the students are reading harder and harder nonfiction books in search of information about the coral reef, intrinsic motivation is being stressed because they're very excited to work with all of the different supplies and textures in creating their representation of a coral reef, and group process is being applied as they work together interacting in teams and small groups, and as a total group to solve problems, make decisions, and complete a joint project. Decisions must be made as a group. Problems are solved as the students work together interacting and creating their creative art project. A definite change comes over the group each time they work together on a group project. Arguments are not allowed and no one person is permitted to make all of the decisions for the group. Everyone's ideas and suggestions are accepted and considered as the coral reef is constructed. Group members also learn not to destroy what someone else has made or to laugh at someone else's contribution. Students work on the coral reef in groups of two or three at a time; therefore, they must protect, workaround, and add on to what previous groups have constructed. The sense of group pride that develops from this project is amazing to watch develop.

Self-Efficacy Brings About Change

Indeed, self-efficacy is an important component of many aspects of your after-school program. Teaching the skills necessary to rebuild self-efficacy leads to academic success. Erasing failure and reestablishing perceptions of success through the teaching of new skills (self-efficacy) bring about greater mental wellness. Being successful and actually learning a new skill (self-efficacy) build motivation.

There is often a bit of confusion over the term self-efficacy, so let us take a moment to clarify this term. Self-efficacy is not the same as self-esteem. Self-efficacy means you believe that you are capable of accomplishing a task—reading a book or working a math problem. Self-efficacy requires learning skills. Self-esteem only means that you feel good about yourself and what you are doing. A student may be in a gang, failing every subject, and plan to help rob the corner grocery store, and yet, have very high self-esteem. This is why I caution you: do not fall for the dangerous premise that the schools subscribe to: high self-esteem will not necessarily help students learn (Baumeister et al. 2005). High self-esteem will not improve group behavior. I can have very high self-esteem while failing every subject, especially if everyone else in my peer group is failing and expects me to fail as well.

Positive self-efficacy, in contrast, does help students learn (Bandura et al. 2001). Rebuilding self-efficacy goes hand in hand with skill-building (Bandura 1997). You cannot have one without the other. I use vowel clustering (Clanton Harpine 2010b) with the students in my program to help rebuild each student's self-efficacy and start them on the road to reading. You must teach skills in order to actually rebuild self-efficacy (Bandura 1986); therefore part of your teaching strategy must include skill-building.

Rebuilding self-efficacy is one of the essential steps in group-centered prevention. Your after-school program must help children rebuild self-efficacy in order to help them overcome academic failure. If you want to bring about change, you must rebuild self-efficacy. Yet, some people confuse curiosity or compliance with self-efficacy. Let's look at an example. A teacher explained to me that her class did an hour of sustained silent reading every afternoon. She explained to me that she arranged a collection of books, some easy and some hard, on a shelf in the back of the room. The books were not stacked, but arranged where the children could see the covers or simply pick up and thumb through a book before making a selection. The teacher knew that I often talked about the importance of self-efficacy and told me one day how pleased she was that her students had changed and were demonstrating their improved self-efficacy because of the books they were selecting and their willingness to sit down and read. It is wonderful to encourage reading, but we cannot say that children demonstrate positive self-efficacy just because they select a harder book to read or actually sit down to read. Before we can claim improvement in self-efficacy, we must look at the situation in which the student was working. Was this a class assignment? Was the student told to select a book? Did the student have any other option than to sit down and read? Compliance with classroom rules is desirable, but does not necessarily indicate improved self-efficacy or change.

The same is true for the book the student selects to read. Just because a student picks up a harder book to read does not necessarily mean improved self-efficacy or new confidence in reading. The harder book may simply have had a more colorful and interesting cover, or there may have been interesting pictures inside the book. Perhaps the title sounded interesting.

We can only claim that we have indeed rebuilt or restored a student's positive self-efficacy when the student is willing to take on a harder task and persist or complete that task because they believe that they truly can. If a student is picking up a book out of curiosity, interest in the title or cover, or because it is a classroom assignment, you cannot claim that this shows improvement in self-efficacy. When a student selects a challenging book without being told to and then chooses to read that book rather than talk on their cell phone or watch TV, then we have a basis to talk about self-efficacy. The student has chosen a hard task (rather than being told to) and the student has chosen to continue that task without extrinsic reward.

The first step in building this kind of self-efficacy is teaching the student the skills necessary for making such a choice. For example, children who cannot read will not pick up a book about coral reefs because they are confident that they can read the book. More likely, the children will pick up the book because they are fascinated by the colorful pictures of coral reefs in the book. Many students learn in school how to pretend to read silently during sustained silent reading sessions; indeed, some are even masters at turning the pages as if they were actually reading; it's not a hard skill. The only way to tell whether the student can actually read the material or not is to have the student read out loud. So, don't confuse curiosity or compliance for self-efficacy. Just because your students may pick up a book when you tell them to at the after-school program, it doesn't mean that they can or that they actually are reading. If we want our after-school program to actually lead to actual change, we must develop self-efficacy fostering strategies into our program.

Building Change into Your After-School Program

Albert Bandura (1995) lists four steps for rebuilding self-efficacy: mastery experiences (skills-training), vicarious experiences (interacting in a positive atmosphere with others), social persuasion (stressing improvement rather than competition), and physiological and emotional states (reducing stress and creating positive experiences). Let us see how these four steps could be applied in an after-school program.

Mastery experiences. Hands-on learning experiences help children experience change while they learn new skills. Hands-on learning is much more effective than just telling students information. One example that I use in my own program is *capturing tricky words*. Yes, children know they have missed the word, but they like the psychological aspect of faulting the word for being tricky rather than their lack of ability. Therefore, I reduce some of the stress of learning a new skill by making a game out of the learning process. The children actually go out to capture

100 tricky (missed) words during one of their activities. This group-centered approach to teaching skills helps reduce stress, erase feelings or perceptions of failure, and helps to rebuild self-efficacy by demonstrating to the child that they can indeed learn new words which thereby increases the child's confidence and belief that they can read and spell. Therefore, the children are willing to go out and tackle new challenges and develop a real interest in reading. Working with hands-on craft projects also teaches a sense of commitment, a desire to complete what you start without giving up or refusing to try. Turning the learning of new skills into a fun hands-on game also makes it easier for children to bounce back from problems or difficulties that arise. Everyone in the group is capturing words; it very quickly becomes the thing to do. So, make it fun to learn.

Vicarious experiences. Students must experience success if they are to rebuild their self-efficacy and change. Group process provides both a modeling and an observation experience for students. The group experience must be totally noncompetitive and very cohesive. We'll talk more about cohesion in a moment, but for now, let's concentrate on the modeling aspect of self-efficacy. The skill-building tasks must be appropriate for the child's abilities, challenging but not beyond the skill level of the student. Children must feel encouraged and challenged but not fear failure or be worried that they will be embarrassed if they cannot accomplish the task. In my program, there are two girls who always want to work together. I encourage individualized instruction, but at the same time, I don't discourage friendship. One girl has a higher skill level but a very difficult time staying focused on a task, while the other girl struggles with the skills but never wavers in her attention to the task. The two girls actually work together very well as a team. They are not always at the same workstation, but I've noticed that, when they are, the girl with attention focusing problems works harder to stay on task so that she can work with her friend. The little girl who struggles with skills works twice as hard so that she can try to keep up with her friend. Is this competition? No, this is constructive modeling (Morgan et al. 1996). When two students are actually observing and modeling the best behavior of the other, the two students are helping each other. It is not competitive, because neither girl is trying to be better than the other. They just enjoy working together. They even help and complement each other. Keeping your program noncompetitive is the best way to foster such vicarious experiences. Encourage students to share, take turns, and help each other.

Social persuasion. For social persuasion to be effective in your after-school program, the students who participate in your program must be able to see their self-improvement. Working in a group can help children who have trouble controlling their actions learn to work in a classroom-like environment. This is particularly true for students who live in low socioeconomic high-risk neighborhoods or for those diagnosed with ADHD (Strayhorn 2002). The movement between eight learning centers helps children learn to exhibit control, so when they return to the classroom they have developed strategies to help them act appropriately (Klingberg et al. 2002). The hands-on creative art interventions enable children to focus on the task, work together cooperatively, and increase academic achievement. I use controlled painting sessions; these sessions are particularly important for students with ADHD or bullying tendencies. There is a group painting project in each of my 12 program packets. These projects teach group skills: interaction, sharing ideas and feelings, compromise, decision-making, problem-solving, control, and work quality. Each project becomes more difficult. *All about Books*, the first theme, has the children paint a cloth costume to represent a character from a book that they have read. Two or three children are allowed to paint at a time. They work at the same table, but each of the children paints his or her own costume. Their first skill is to learn to share paint because I put out only one container of paint in each color. Students must share and take turns. For the second theme, *Outer Space Exploration*, students work together on one cloth to make one large picture of the Milky Way galaxy. Again, they must take turns, but this time, they must decide as a group (decision-making) how to paint their galaxy to make it look like the picture. By the time they get to the *Ocean* theme, which is the third 12-session theme, the group is research-ing, making decisions as a group, solving problems, and working together to make one large coral reef. The excitement of the project stimulates interaction; the neces-sity of having to work together cooperatively generates cohesion. Hands-on group-centered creative art projects help you mold group process and enable you to lead your group members toward lasting interpersonal change.

Physiological and emotional states. Children's perceptions of their own ability, their self-efficacy, are derived from their previous experiences, both good and bad. A student's experience at school in the classroom with the teacher and with fellow classmates has a strong influence on how the student's self-efficacy develops. Parents and their perspective on learning and education also influence the student's self-efficacy. A group-centered after-school prevention program can provide a safe, noncompetitive learning environment where students can work in mastering skills from the classroom at their own pace. This is extremely important when as we dis-cussed earlier you are working with students who may have learning disabilities. No two students are the same; therefore, your after-school program must provide a structure where students can feel accepted and motivated to learn. Structured skill-building activities which offer challenge and real-world relevance in a positive, supportive group atmosphere lead to healthy psychological development and con-structive change and offer the best atmosphere for academic improvement in after-school programming (Hill 2008; Shernoff 2010).

Step 5: Designing a Learning Center to Bring About Change

What type of changes are you hoping to bring about through your program?

How does your overall group structure use group process to bring about change?

What kind of mastery experiences will you create for the children in your after-school program?

How would you create vicarious experiences?

How will you encourage social persuasion?

How would your activities support the physiological and emotional states of your students?

What type of group-centered creative art interventions will you use to foster the development of cohesion in your program?

Step 5, Design Example

Types of changes. A group-centered after-school prevention program must include skill-building. Skill-building is linked with academic change, but it is not enough to just teach skills. If our after-school program is to be successful, we must also help the children overcome negative perceptions, failure, and any problems that they confronted in the classroom. We cannot rebuild self-efficacy if failure lurks in our students' minds. We cannot simply tell students the answers to a math problem or help them answer comprehension questions for a story and expect them to automatically feel competent. Students must experience the change in order for change to actually occur. I rely on learning centers with hands-on intrinsic motivators and intensive skill-building interwoven into a cohesive group-centered structure designed to prevent academic failure and foster psychological well-being. My

Reading Orienteering Club is more than just a reading program. I want to change not only how the child reads but also how the child approaches life.

Using group process to bring about change. I use group process through small groups at the learning centers, with designated painting groups, and through total group activities, such as the weekly TV show or puppet plays which involve everyone. Creating activities which generate interaction and teaching the children to work together cooperatively thereby build cohesion and change into my program.

Mastery experiences. During the *Ocean* theme, the children make a giant fish puppet; the children go out in search of 64 *tricky* words (a tricky word is a word that the child does not know). They make a fish scale for each tricky word, and then use these scales to make a giant paper bag fish puppet. The children can lift the scales, practice the tricky words, and also use the giant fish as a puppet for their puppet play and TV show. Each time the child finds a tricky word, they use the *4-steps* to learn that word: (1) say the word out loud, (2) spell the word by writing it correctly in their notebook, (3) give a definition or look up the meaning in the dictionary, and (4) use the word correctly in a sentence. In this way, the children actually work with the words they do not know and have a chance to learn them. The *4-step* process is essential to mastering or learning new words. Capturing tricky words helps children increase their spelling skills, reading skills, sight word proficiency, phoneme awareness, and comprehension through knowing the actual meaning of words. Working together in a group where everyone is capturing tricky words encourages interaction, acceptance, and eventually cohesion. There is no competition and no one feels bad when he or she misses a word. Therefore, the perception of failure falls away and is replaced by the challenge of learning and capturing new tricky words.

Vicarious experience. A creative art mascot called *Ollie Octopus* (Clanton Harpine 2013a) is introduced to the children through stories where *Ollie Octopus* is constantly getting in trouble. Each learning center has a different story about *Ollie Octopus*. The children are then challenged to write stories telling how to change *Ollie's* behavior. Sometimes they write an ending for a story telling how *Ollie* could get out of trouble or find a friend or talk with someone about a problem. *Ollie Octopus* becomes the modeling example for changing behavior. As the stories begin to tell how *Ollie Octopus* changed his behavior and became happier, the group members also begin to demonstrate ways that they can change their behavior. Stories, craft projects, puppet plays, and a pop-up book revolve around this new character and help students learn to reflect upon their own behavior and how it could be changed for the better.

Social persuasion. Painting is a wonderful hands-on activity that helps children forget their problems and fears. Sometimes I use painting sessions to encourage group interaction and problem-solving. At other times, I will use painting sessions to teach a particular lesson. With one group, I had everyone sit in a circle around the table. The cloth to be painted was in the center of the table. Each child was allowed to paint but only one at a time. I wanted to emphasize controlling actions and impulsive behavior. Children often become excited when painting; therefore, I used a fun activity to practice control. I called children forward to paint one at a time depending upon how well they were modeling the desired behavior of waiting quietly for a turn. Children were also given a specific painting assignment. I worked with approximately ten children at a time. No one was left out, but the children did have to wait for a turn. I gave each child an assignment. Paint six blades of grass, three thumbprint flowers, two trees, or six daisies. I demonstrated how to paint each flower, and the children were asked to mimic the flower demonstrated. I used very simple handprint tulips and thumbprint daisy flowers that all children could easily make. Enforcing a specific structure on the painting activity demonstrated to the children that (1) they could control their behavior and (2) they could produce a quality painting of which they were all very proud.

Physiological and emotional states. I use a step system in my program. Everyone starts at step one, a very early (vowel clustered) reading level. I make sure that all of my students can successfully read the books or material that I place at Step 1. I measure the progress at steps by having the children capture tricky words. If the student captures five tricky words at Step 1, then they use the *4-step method* described earlier to practice the captured words. After which, they go on to the next workstation. If the student does not capture any words at Step 1, they progress to Step 2. The stories at Step 2 are naturally a bit harder. Again, they capture words. If the student captures five tricky words at Step 2, they use the *4-step method* and then proceed on to the next station. If the student does not capture any tricky words at Step 2, they move up to Step 3. Step 3 is always a challenge. Again, they read to capture tricky words. If I have a student who does not capture tricky words at Step 3, they get to go for the super challenge. In other words, I break down the reading levels so that each student can read at their own ability level without being embarrassed. It's a fun game. The children enjoy moving up the steps and capturing the words. Since everyone starts at Step 1, it's impossible for anyone to keep up with who is reading at which level. Plus, my program is very fast-paced and is jam-packed with eight wonderful hands-on workstations; so the children do not have time to sit around and get into trouble or tease each other. Everyone is busy trying to finish his or her projects. There are always daily and weekly hands-on projects. Some are very easy, and some are a bit challenging. The focus is always on building skills.

Group-centered creative art interventions. Intensive skill-building instruction is enhanced through creative art interventions. Hands-on creative interventions can be simple or complicated. My projects range from something as simple as *Sandy the Panda* which has children simply trace a bear pattern, color the black markings for the panda by looking at a picture, cut two notches for a word strip, and then make a word strip of tricky words to slide through the notches. This is a very simple project, but it helps children practice their vowel sounds. Projects in my program can be individual projects such as a puppet or a group project such as painting a puppet stage or planning a TV show. Making puppets motivates children to write puppet plays and to practice reading out loud which improves fluency. You can have the children follow step-by-step directions to make a sea turtle marionette puppet (one of my harder projects) or you can give children an empty plastic water bottle and a table filled with paper, cloth, buttons, and other creative items. Then, tell the children to create a puppet and write a puppet play for their puppet. Creativity is endless and can be shaped to fit what you hope to achieve with the group. Use creative art activities as a teaching tool and intervention tool to work with your group members. Group-centered creative art interventions can help you bring about change in your after-school prevention program.

Real-World Applications

Observational Extensions

If possible, observe someone who uses creative art interventions. If you cannot find such a group, try an experiment with your neighborhood children. First, try to teach the children about butterflies by simply explaining what a butterfly is and how it flies. Ask how many understand. Second, give the children a simple butterfly pattern to trace, crayons, and a stick to glue their butterfly onto. While the children are coloring their butterflies, give the same information about how a butterfly flies. Demonstrate by gluing butterflies to sticks and showing how the wings move up and down. Once everyone has his or her butterfly completed, now, ask again how many understand. Getting children involved in the learning process increases concentration and application of information.

Troubleshooting Checklists for Organizing a New After-School Program

1. Are you applying the four steps for self-efficacy in the development of your learning center workstations?
2. Do your workstations encourage interaction and cohesion?
3. Do you use group-centered creative art interventions each day in your program?

A Ready-to-Use Group-Centered Learning Center Intervention, Designing a Learning Center to Bring About Change: On the Air

This is an example to illustrate how to use the make-believe TV show at a workstation. The instructions give a sample of only one day and only one workstation. Many of our TV show projects take more than one session, particularly if the students are making a puppet or writing a puppet play. I videotape the TV shows because the children really enjoy seeing their performance. You will need to find books at your students' reading levels. This particular project is designed to be used near the end of the year when most students are at least reading beginning-level books. If you cannot find appropriate books to match the needs of your students, write short stories for your beginning readers. You can even write a simple fact on an index card and show these cards at Step 1. Beginning readers may only want to write one simple sentence about their person in history. Make sure that Step 1 is appropriate for all students so that everyone is included.

Another way to include early readers is to have several students report about the same person. Early readers might give a one-sentence statement for their report, followed by a more complete report by a more advanced reader:

Reporter #1: John Glenn was the first American to eat applesauce in outer space.

Reporter #2: John Glenn used a tube, similar to a tube of toothpaste, to eat in outer space.

Reporter #3: John Glenn was the first American to orbit the earth. [Then, the report could go on with more details.]

ON THE AIR

Step 1: Welcome to the TV studio. Remember that our goal is to work together as a group to put together a TV show to be presented at the end of our session today. The script is ready and waiting. Your job is to be an On-the-Spot reporter. On the table we have a collection of books about famous Americans. Select a book that you would like to report on. Start at Step 1 and see if you find a book that you like.

Step 2: As you read, look for answers to the questions: Who? What? When? Where? and Why? Your workstation helper will help you. Take notes as your read.

Step 3: Write your news report using the information that you learned from your book. Remember, we never copy from a book. We read, and then write using our own words, and reporters give only the facts.

Step 4: Have your workstation helper edit your story before it goes on the air.

Step 5: Practice reading your report. Remember to speak loud and clear when you are on the air. Sign up to be one of our on-the-spot reporters today. When you have finished your report, try the challenge step or go to the next station.

ARE YOU READY FOR A CHALLENGE?

Challenge Step: We need two announcers and one stage director for our TV show today. The stage director will help tell the on-the-spot reporters when it's their time to speak. Practice the skit and be ready.

Famous Americans

Stage Director: Quiet on the set. We are on the air in 3…2…1… [point to announcer]

Announcer #1: Welcome to our show today. We are talking about famous Americans, and we're glad you decided to join us.

Announcer #2: We sent our On the Spot reporters out far and wide to see how many famous Americans they could find.

Announcer #1: I can hardly wait to see who they've discovered. Let's get started.

On the Spot Reporter #1:

Announcer #2: Famous Americans include women too. Who can tell us about a famous woman in history?

Announcer #1: I knew she was going to say that.

On the Spot Reporter #2:

[Include other reports. It will depend on how many On the Spot reporters that you have today. Arrange reports so that everyone gets a turn. Then close the show.]

Announcer #1: Well, that was certainly interesting.

Announcer #2: See, I told you there were lots of famous women.

Announcer #1: I never doubted it for a second.

Announcer #2: Listening to all of those reports makes me want to go out and do some reading too. I think I am going to wander over to the library and see if I can't find an interesting book to read. Are you coming?

Announcer #1: Sounds like a good idea. Maybe you'd like to check out a book at your library? There are shelves of books about famous Americans. Go check it out!

Chapter 6
Interaction in a Year-Long Program

He was a third grader who had been retained twice in school for reading failure. Shy with other students, he was talkative around adults. His classroom teacher said that he refused to talk with other students or participate in class discussions. He sat by himself during snack time, and then cooperatively walked to his first learning center workstation. He was quickly joined by two other students. He talked to the workstation helper, but never to the two students working at the same station with him. He avoided most students, and they avoided him. This pattern continued as he went from workstation to workstation, until he came to a workstation that required a group decision. There was a list of snacks; the group had to decide which snack was the healthiest and why. Each student was first required to vote on their choice for healthiest snack; the group then discussed the pros and cons of each choice and made a group decision. This activity, in effect, forced interactive discussion and group decision-making. The other group members listened to the third grader when he talked, especially when he reminded the others that they had to consider calories and fat content in making a healthy snack choice. As the third grader moved to the next workstation, he seemed a little braver and actually started a conversation with one of the other students. This continued and after several months, the third grader was sitting with others during snack time, talking with others while he worked at the workstations, and even volunteered to be one of the three puppeteers for the weekly TV show. It did not happen immediately, but structured learning center workstations designed to initiate positive, constructive interaction helped this student overcome his reluctance to get involved in a group.

Every group interacts. It is actually impossible for a group not to interact. Even if a group of students are sitting in a room being totally silent, that is a form of interaction. Interaction involves influencing others or being influenced by others. Silence in a group is influential. Interaction is like communication in that it is impossible not to communicate. If a student walks into a room and refuses to talk to anyone, that is a form of communication. By refusing to interact and communicate with others, the student is communicating that the student is either shy and unsure of how to make friends, feels superior to other group members, fears group involvement, or has

E. Clanton Harpine, *After-School Prevention Programs for At-Risk Students: Promoting Engagement and Academic Success*, DOI 10.1007/978-1-4614-7416-6_6, © Springer Science+Business Media New York 2013

other personal concerns which keep the student from getting involved. Such inability or refusal to interact with others is a form of interaction, even though no words were spoken. The student alters the development of the group when the student fails to interact or participate. Any form of disruption to the development of group process, from shyness to blatant refusal, stifles constructive interaction.

Interaction is essential for cohesion. Such a disruption in the normal development of your after-school group can have devastating effects. You cannot build a successful after-school program without cohesion. Cohesion is essential for development, improvement, and change, but not all interaction leads to cohesion.

Stages of Development

Interaction involves verbally what is said, vocally how it is said, and the nonverbal way in which it is said. Interaction begins on the very first day, the first minute your students arrive, but you cannot simply turn children and teenagers loose in a group setting and assume that they will just naturally gravitate toward cohesive interaction. It doesn't happen. Your after-school group must work through five basic stages of development before it can become a cohesive, well-functioning group: early formation or getting acquainted, chaotic juggling for leadership and compliance, acceptance of structure, building relationships, and, only then, cohesion (Posthuma 2002). There is not a set number of days that your group needs to work through each phase. The development of your after-school group will depend upon (1) the students participating in your program and the group dynamics or way those students work together in a group and (2) the way(s) in which you structure interaction between group members or the way you use group process to achieve your group goals.

Getting acquainted. Most after-school programs start with a flurry of activity. It is best if you can take care of permission forms, health forms, and any pretesting before the first day. Children and teens are nervous when they start a new program. Absolutely never start by reading off a list of rules. Start with action. Have workstations set up and ready before the children arrive. Move the children into your learning center workstation structure as soon as possible. This creates positive interaction.

Leadership and compliance. You will not have difficulty realizing that some students must test the boundaries and challenge your authority. Do not let this phase monopolize your group or continue for too long, but realize that it is an inevitable part of group process. Your group will not be able to skip this developmental step, and yes, such juggling for positions and recognition results in a bit of chaos as everyone settles into the program. Do not give into the temptation to sit everyone down in a circle of chairs and lecture or hand out worksheets and demand quiet work time. Stay with your learning center structure and work through this phase of your group's development. Each of your learning center workstations should stress not only self-efficacy and skill-building but also interpersonal skills. This will help. Keep the learning centers positive; handle discipline problems individually away from the learning center. For example, while studying the EA vowel sound, you might emphasize the word *team*. The workstation could have tricky practice words to capture and also say, "When we work together helping each other, we work as a team. Being a member of our ROC team doesn't mean competition. Our team here at the *Reading Orienteering Club* means that we go out of our way to help each other, say kind words, and never hurt someone else's feelings. Welcome to the team. Write in your notebook five ways that you can show team spirit by being nice to someone here at the *Reading Orienteering Club* today. Then, go out and practice being nice to others." No, the positive approach does not work with everyone. Some students need to be reminded that there are consequences to their actions. We will talk more about how to handle behavioral problems in Chap. 7.

Acceptance of structure. When the students begin to accept and work with your group structure—learning centers, TV show, or whatever structure you are using—then you will see them begin to settle down and work. At this point rebuilding self-efficacy becomes very important. As the group grows and develops, the group participants must also be growing, developing, and working toward change. It is crucial that your after-school program uses positive, constructive, cohesion-building interaction. You want to bring all of the factors that we have talked about into this phase of your group's development—self-efficacy, intrinsic motivation, 11 curative factors, change, and interaction which leads to cohesion.

Building relationships. Once you have your group working and striving toward change, interpersonal development comes to the forefront of your program as participants begin to analyze and evaluate how they act toward others. Working together in small groups and on total group projects becomes very important at this point. Build interaction into workstations. In my program, group painting, puppet plays, and the make-believe TV show provide opportunities for students to work together in groups. They have to make decisions, plan, write, and solve problems together as a group. I reinforce that we are a team, not a competitive team or a sport team, but a team where everyone works together supporting and helping each other. Children and teens are naturally drawn to the team concept. I continue to emphasize that we are a supportive team; we help each other and show that we care.

Cohesion. As you pull all the elements of a successful after-school program together, you should see your group becoming more cohesive. It will not happen overnight; it will not happen automatically. This is why group structure is so important. I use learning center workstations because they give me the most flexibility to provide for the individual needs of my students and the program's group structure needs.

Unintentional Disruptions

There are always disruptions or concerns which must be dealt with in a group program. A student's refusal to speak nonverbally communicates the student's refusal to become involved with the group. As with the student in our opening story, you may at first say, "What's the problem? The student is being quiet and going off and working without causing any trouble." The student's refusal to get involved is a form of disruptive interaction for self and for the group. Disruptive interaction is a barrier to cohesion. It is your job to build constructive interaction into your after-school program so that all students become actively involved and cooperative. You cannot build a cohesive program if every student is not involved. As mentioned in our opening example, build interaction into your learning center workstations so that students must talk together, make decisions, and solve problems together as a group.

One year I had a student who was very cooperative and very eager to learn to read, but she had no desire to be a part of the group, to talk or work with others, or to work in teams or small groups. I announced at the beginning of a session that today would be teamwork day, and that everyone would work with a partner. I paired the students into teams so that I could control the combined group dynamics. I paired this particular student with one of my harder working, older students. The two girls worked well together, and by the end of the session, I noticed that my reluctant student was more willing to talk and participate.

Shy and reluctant students must be brought into the group as full participating members before you have any hope of achieving a cohesive group structure. You cannot simply tell shy students to talk; you must show them how. Acceptance and trust play a major role.

Intentional Disruptions

A more common form of disruptive interaction is frequently found in after-school programs: bullying, teasing, laughing at, making fun of, or belittling others in the group. Such behavior is totally unacceptable and must be stopped the minute it starts. Your group cannot achieve cohesion until every single member is accepted and feels accepted by the group. We will speak more directly to behavior problems in Chap. 7. Our goal in this chapter is to illustrate how an after-school program can structure interaction in order to bring about interaction that becomes positive for the group and for the individual students participating in the after-school program. Sometimes, when educators use the term "being positive," they give the mistaken impression that "being positive" will solve all of your discipline problems. Never. I totally believe in being positive, but you cannot maintain a positive group atmosphere if one student is being teased or made fun of. Ignoring such behavior or contending that simply "being positive" will stop such belittling behavior is foolish. If you want to have a cohesive after-school program, you must control behavior problems. Problems and conflicts will always occur and you must deal with them so that they are not allowed to draw away from constructive interaction, but in this chapter, I want to keep our focus on positive interaction.

Group Atmosphere Is Important

If we are to build constructive interaction into our after-school program, we must create a group atmosphere of trust—no bullying, no teasing, and no laughing at other group members. Each and every group member must feel safe and accepted. This is the first requirement for constructive interaction. To create this atmosphere of trust, group members must feel attracted to (desiring to be a part of) or develop a special bond (feeling of acceptance) with your after-school group. Your after-school program must become a group that group participants want to be a part of and receive support from, and a group in which they believe that other students actually care about them. False praise or shallow, one-sided, unsubstantiated praise will not encourage shy students to get involved. They need to believe that others will listen to them, help them, and even teach them the skills that they need to overcome their problems. Shy students need to feel safe in the group, but they also need to feel as if others in the group truly want to be involved with them. In reading, for example, students need to believe that vowel clustering can help them learn to read. This belief is supported when they see themselves reading, sometimes for the very first time. Once at-risk students begin learning to read, they are then ready to begin working on other changes, such as group behavior and making friends. Rebuild self-efficacy first so that you have a positive skill-base to work from. Then work on relationships.

How to Build Constructive Interaction into a Year-Long After-School Program

The first thing to remember is that building constructive interaction is not a one-time incident. You must continue building positive, constructive interaction into your after-school program all year long—from start to finish. You must also strive to make sure that each learning center and each group activity works toward the goal of positive interaction and group cohesion.

Learning Centers

Learning centers generate constructive interaction. By having students travel around to eight different learning center workstations, I am constantly formulating small groups, remixing those groups, and formulating new groups. This encourages students to interact and work with others. There is always someone new and different to work with at each workstation. Students move individually to workstations; they do not move as a group. Moving students by groups stifles interaction and motivation. Never assign groups and never move students between workstations in designated groups, unless you have a specific purpose for formulating special groups (I'll talk more about this in Chap. 7).

Learning centers allow you to individualize instruction to meet the learning needs of your individual participants. Step-by-step learning center instructions allow you to help students master the skills needed to rebuild self-efficacy. For example, in my program, each learning center teaches *vowel clustering* through a hands-on creative art project which encourages and motivates children to keep working through eight different learning center workstations. At the same time, the learning centers stress at least 1 of the 11 therapeutic factors of change and strive to move the group closer to achieving cohesion through constructive interactive group activities. Cohesion doesn't happen on the first day. It takes months of hard work to create a cohesive after-school group. Let's look at an example.

My students make a coral reef pop-up book. It is one of the more complicated books that they make, and it is therefore presented about two-thirds of the way through the year. By that point, students have been introduced to all of the vowel clusters, but continuous review is still very important. They spend several sessions making the coral reef pop-up book. Each learning center reviews a vowel sound and offers a pattern that students must trace in order to make their book. There are pop-up coral reef pieces, an underwater deep-sea cave, swimming fish, and then an octopus, squid, or sea turtle (student's choice) which pops-up inside the cave. Tracing and cutting patterns provide excellent fine motor skill training. Children who struggle to write are more inclined to practice their fine motor skills by tracing and cutting than they are by simply practicing handwriting. This does not mean that handwriting practice is not important. It is, but you must first help students develop fine motor control before they are ready to practice and improve their handwriting.

To make their book, children must read, research, and add nonfiction facts about coral reefs and the sea creatures which they have chosen to add to their book. The children are also challenged to write a fictional story about the creatures in their pop-up book. Throughout the 12-session *Ocean* theme, the students also make puppets and write puppet plays about *Ollie Octopus, Squishy the Squid,* and *Seymour the Sea Turtle.* Each puppet's name emphasizes a vowel sound. Each puppet also focuses on a behavior. *Ollie Octopus* is always misbehaving, so the students have to write puppet plays that help him learn how to behave. *Squishy the Squid* has a bad temper and goes out of his way to cause trouble for others. *Seymour the Sea Turtle* is very shy. Puppet and puppet plays help students reflect upon their own behavior and how they might change and act differently in the group. This can all be accomplished through learning centers by writing learning center instructions that bring about these group accomplishments. I do not introduce these characters at the beginning of the year because my students are not ready to work on interpersonal relationships. At the beginning of the year, I stress rebuilding self-efficacy. Once students begin to see success, they are ready to consider behavioral change.

Learning centers are an excellent method for adding positive, constructive interaction to your after-school program. You can create group projects that lead to group change. Learning center workstations with step-by-step directions give you the most flexibility and enable you to meet the needs of each individual student.

Remember to keep students moving individually at their own pace between work-stations. This freedom of movement enhances individualized instruction and also encourages group interaction through the mixing and remixing of small groups. This is a very important factor in the development of your group. If you want your group to become cohesive, you must foster positive group interaction.

Puppet Plays

You want the members of your after-school program to feel so comfortable with each other that they are willing to share their thoughts, ideas, and feelings with other group members. A group-centered after-school prevention program is not a therapy group and does not strive for self-disclosure of personal problems. Such disclosure is better left to therapy sessions. A group-centered after-school prevention program does strive for change though and to share feelings about working together. We are striving for change academically, motivationally, and for personal growth and development which leads to psychological wellness and a happier well-being. Puppet plays serve as an excellent means of generating group interaction which leads to personal growth and change. Puppet plays require cooperation and interaction. They fulfill self-efficacy needs by encouraging mastery of reading skills and provide opportunities for group members to work together cooperatively. Puppet plays encourage intrinsic motivation through the making of puppets, the writing of skits, and the presentation of the puppet play.

At the end of my after-school program each year, my students present an hour-long program. Parents and families are invited. The children spend weeks making puppets, writing puppet skits, practicing in small groups, and even making special props or decorations for the program. We videotape the program as part of their make-believe TV show. Every single student is involved, and they work in small groups and as a total group to get ready for their production. I have found that it actually works better to have the children work in groups of three or four for a puppet play. When you try to have one long play with 30 children involved, it becomes too complicated and disorganized. Therefore, try a series of short plays on different topics. In this way, small groups can work together to write and develop their own ideas. I also separate puppet readers from puppeteers. For example, I'll have one group of three children practice with and be the puppeteers for a group of three who have written a puppet play and made puppets about pollution. The two groups of three will practice so that the readers are ready to read in front of an audience and the puppeteers practice so that they will know when to display the puppet in keeping with the action. Then, the groups switch. Those who were puppet readers become the puppeteers for the other group as they read and practice their play. In this way, each child gets to be both a puppeteer and a reader. Young children or even teenagers are often not able to manage reading a script while they manipulate a puppet to respond to the actions in the puppet play. Therefore, I divide the work tasks between two small groups and increase group interaction for my overall program.

Action Stories

If the children in your after-school program are unable to read a puppet skit, but you would like to have an intervention for increasing interaction, I suggest using *action stories*. I use the *Camp Sharigan* (Clanton Harpine 2010a) intensive 2-hour-a-day, 5-day reading clinic for a weeklong kickoff for my *Reading Orienteering Club* each year. *Camp Sharigan* is filled with action stories. Even though my *Reading Orienteering Club* after-school program meets only twice a week throughout the year, *Camp Sharigan's* weeklong emphasis gives a very strong first week; an exciting kickoff week raises the motivational level, and encourages the children to get excited about reading.

One of the action stories from *Camp Sharigan*, "Noisy the Car," is such a favorite with the children that we refer to it all year long. Noisy is a very impulsive character. When Noisy starts to read a sign for directions, he is so impulsive that he reads the first sentence and then charges off saying, "Oh, I know all about that. I don't need to read that sign." Naturally, he should have read the sign, and Noisy ends up having to go back and reread the entire sign. "Noisy the Car" is told with all kinds of animal sounds (dog, owl, cow, cat). As the reader reads the story, a designated child responds with the noise for that animal as the animal's name is used in the story. This helps children listen, work together as a group, and learn to take turns. Every child gets a turn to be a character in one of the action stories, but a single story may not have 30 different sounds. Taking turns and being patient is always a good lesson. Therefore, action stories teach group skills, encourage positive group interaction and reading and listening skills, and also teach children important rules—you need to read every single learning center workstation sign and read it completely, one step at a time. When children seem to be rushing on a project, I will ask, "Who remembers what "Noisy the Car" taught us?" Even if it's the last month of the program, the reply is always, "to read the sign, the entire workstation sign." Action stories can be fun; they can teach, and help you initiate interaction, especially on the first day of a new program. So, keep action stories in mind when you're trying to figure out how to get started on that first day. You may write your own stories or find books at the library which include animal sounds.

TV Studio

A make-believe TV show is an excellent way to generate interaction in your after-school program. All ages love the make-believe TV studio, but the older elementary students and teenagers work best in the TV studio. Very simple puppet plays can be written for any age, even vowel-clustered puppet plays; therefore, everyone can be a puppet reader. With a TV (make-believe) broadcast, it's a little more difficult. All ages participate in the TV show, as puppeteers or by reading simple stories, but the

On-the-Spot reporters who research nonfiction books and write factual news stories are usually my older students or stronger readers. It's the challenge step at the workstations.

As the children's skills improve across the year, more and more children sign up to be reporters; therefore, it serves as a motivational step as well. Again, using the concept of step-by-step progress is very motivating. Everyone is included with the first TV show; even if they cannot read or do not even know the alphabet, they become a puppeteer and a participant in the TV show. I use *Andy the Ant* for their first puppet play. Andy is a simple puppet to make, and all of the children are excited to be ants at the anthill. As the children progress and learn to read, I write puppet skits for first-grade, second-grade, and third-grade readers. I naturally do not put grade designations on the skit, but give each character a name and assign readers by ability. Early readers are excited to be included and able to step up and be a puppet reader. Those who are not reading in the puppet play are not discouraged though, because every single student enjoys being a puppeteer. There is something about holding the puppet in your hand that makes the day very exciting. Working together as a group to make sure that everyone is included in the puppet play, even on the first day, reemphasizes the importance of acceptance and cohesion and the development of our group. Puppets generate motivation and encourage positive group interaction.

Service Projects

Even my youngest children participate in service projects. One of our favorite projects is to cook Thanksgiving dinner for a needy family. Yes, we make the sweet potatoes, pumpkin pie, cookies, bread, and anything else that can be made ahead. The children plan the menu, decorate a box(s) to deliver the dinner in, and make a special pop-up card that says Happy Thanksgiving. My program meets in a church and we have access to a kitchen, but, even if you cannot cook in your program, the children can mix and prepare food items that you can then take home and bake. Planning a service project can be a great way to teach decision-making and problem-solving, and to generate positive group interaction. Naturally, there are many service projects that do not involve cooking; this is just one example. Service projects are excellent and work with all ages, but especially with teenagers. Make sure that your project involves something more than just collecting money or collecting cans of food. Service projects which require little work also give fewer dividends to those engaged in the service. Children and teens need hands-on involvement.

Let's turn to the design phase now and see how to put these ideas into practice. Remember, workspace is provided for you to jot down your ideas on how you plan to generate interaction in your after-school program. I discuss in the design example how I answered each question in formulating my own program design.

Step 6: Designing a Learning Center to Encourage Interaction

What will you do in your after-school program to generate positive, constructive group interaction?

How will the group's needs for interaction support the group's needs for self-efficacy?

Will your strategies for increasing group interaction involve intrinsic motivation?

Will your strategies for increasing group interaction help support your efforts to incorporate the 11 therapeutic factors for personal change and improvement?

How will your group efforts to increase interaction lead to cohesion in your program?

Step 6, Design Example

To generate positive interaction. Just as pop-up books are one of my most successful intrinsic motivators, painting puppet stages generates the most interaction. Everyone wants to paint, but each of my painting assignments has a different objective. It is never just paint whatever you want. Sometimes I have very controlled painting when I want to stress focus, control, and group effort. Other times, I encourage group decision-making as part of the painting project. The children painted a fall puppet stage with a lake surrounded by cabins and trees with their fall colors. My instructions were that it must be a total group project; everyone must work together and be included. I taught a few simple painting skills such as painting with sand and painting with sponges to give different effects. They worked on this project for several weeks. They drew a paper sketch before they actually started painting. It was emphasized from the beginning that only polite drawings and suggestions would be accepted; I also retained the right to veto anything that I deemed rude or inappropriate. Each person added to the sketch. Students were not allowed to take anything away or write over anyone else's contribution. I wanted to teach respect for other people's ideas. I also wanted this to be a painting that every single group member contributed to. Once the sketch was complete and everyone was satisfied, the painting began. When we paint as a group, we always start at the left side and paint toward the right so that there is always a clean place for the next person who comes to the workstation to paint. This also meant that since the children were working from a group drawing, sometimes students were painting ideas other than their own. It was a group project. Students constantly stopped and talked about how the painting was progressing, how well they were matching the drawing, and if everyone's ideas were being included. When the painting was complete, each child wrote a story about the scene that they had painted. Some told about geese returning to the lake, and others wrote about hikers in the woods. One little girl wrote about the lonely cabin that no one lived in. The painting project served as a writing prompt. Writing stories provided an opportunity to practice grammatical sentence structure, spelling, and then naturally reading the stories out loud for that week's TV show. The group was noticeably more cohesive after working together on this painting project. They were also very proud of what they had created, and they learned how to fix mistakes. When something didn't turn out exactly as they wanted, instead of getting mad, they learned how to blend it in with the rest of the painting and make everything work out—truly an intrinsic interactive project.

Using interaction to support self-efficacy. The EA vowel combination is used to make seven different vowel sounds. The children make a large paper heart to help them practice and learn these seven sounds (self-efficacy). All eight workstations work toward the completion of this project. At one station, they learn the EA sound as used in the word *heart*. They trace and cut two large paper hearts. Then to make the heart puffy, two students must work together to stuff and seal the hearts with scrap paper. These are not prearranged teams, just interaction between whoever is at the learning center at that time. This gives the students opportunities to work with different group members. Students then proceed on around the learning centers individually capturing tricky EA words to decorate their large heart. Each tricky word is placed on the back of a small paper heart. The hearts are then glued in place so that students may lift and practice the tricky words that they have captured. As work progresses, another workstation asks students to help their neighbor place a crepe paper edging on their heart. Again, this is a two-person job. Students are once again asked to work with whoever is at the learning center, thereby setting up an interactive situation. You can build interaction into your workstation directions while continuing your focus on self-efficacy, intrinsic motivation, and the 11 therapeutic factors. The focus on interaction does not take away from your learning and counseling goals.

Interaction and intrinsic motivation. All of my children and teenagers are enthralled with making pop-up books. Many commercial pop-up books require that an artist draw pictures that pop-up. I am not an artist; therefore, we rely on shapes—houses, rockets, coral reefs, caves, animals, and trees. In the *Protect the Environment* 12-session packet used in my after-school program, the children make a pop-up book displaying several different kinds of trees in the forest. This book takes several weeks to make, and the children read a story about each tree as they make their book. They also write their own story which emphasizes comprehension of what they've read. The books and stories are then presented at the weekly make-believe TV show. Although making a pop-up book is a somewhat individualized project (read, trace, cut, glue in place, and write), I wanted this project to go one step further. As the students finished their pop-up book, they were placed in groups of three and given the assignment to write a puppet play for three tree puppets. They were to use information that they had read at the workstations while making their pop-up book. Often, they had to go back, check, and reread about a certain tree to get the facts straight. Combining pop-up books and puppets into one project made for a very intrinsically stimulating project and yet it still fulfilled all the needs for self-efficacy, interaction, cohesion, and the 11 therapeutic factors. The children were truly working together in cooperative groups.

The 11 therapeutic factors and interaction. I stress blending the 11 therapeutic factors into my workstation activities. I make sure that each learning center workstation has both learning and counseling included. One of the concerns in my program is to also teach about healthy snacks. Healthy eating encourages learning; fats and sugary foods make learning more difficult. I use empty food boxes to show the children how to read the ingredient and nutrition labels. In one of our early sessions, while the children are studying and practicing the vowel sounds for the letter A, I have them check several food boxes to look for the ingredient BHA (a carcinogen often found in children's sugary cereals). They read a short fact sheet on the dangers of BHA, and talk as a group about the consequences of making unhealthy snack choices. The children are then allowed to make a healthy snack using an apple slice, carrot stick, or piece of a banana. Each of these foods' names uses the *a sound*. The children add peanut butter and raisins; raisins use another *a sound*. While everyone is munching on their snack, the workstation helper reads the next step which explains that there are also consequences to our words and actions. The directions go on to explain that sometimes we hurt other people's feelings through the words we speak or the way in which we talk to others. The directions then ask the group to make a list of kind words that would not hurt anyone's feelings. This is a group project but everyone writes the final list in his or her notebook. Then, they are asked to go and share ten kind words with others in the group today. They are reminded that there are consequences to saying mean and hateful words; so we are only going out to say kind words. This workstation includes two group discussions: (1) a discussion over BHA and (2) a discussion over kind words to say. I do not have the students make a list of mean and hateful words; I stress only kind words. This learning center workstation imparts information about BHA and allows students to practice modeling and acting kindly toward others which strengthens cohesion and interpersonal learning as they experience the reactions of others to their kind words.

Interaction which leads to cohesion. Planning puppet plays and TV shows are two of my central cohesion-building interventions, but it is often the steps that lead up to the puppet play and TV show that enable these activities to enhance cohesion. For example, I created Fancy the Race Car to help the students think about what it means to work together in a group. Fancy is a race car that thinks only about what he wants—to win the race. Each learning center workstation has a *vowel-clustered* story about Fancy for the children to read, tricky words to practice and capture (word strips filled with tricky words are used to decorate the race car), an eight-piece paper race car (made from recycled materials) in which they must travel to all eight workstations to assemble, and eight Fancy the Race Car stories which they must write an ending for. In some of the stories, Fancy is very self-centered and can think only of what he wants—to win. The children must write a story explaining to Fancy that it's okay if he doesn't win.

Other stories mention that racing involves being part of a team and working with others. Still another story encourages students to write and tell how others feel when *Fancy* does win and goes around bragging. The children then convert their stories into puppet plays and work in small groups to present puppet plays having their car characters talk and share their feelings about winning and not winning, bragging and not bragging, and most of all, thinking of others. When children work with interpersonal concepts in the form of stories and puppet plays, they are more likely to implement such concepts, particularly when these interpersonal concepts are being stressed each and every day in your after-school program. When you write learning center instructions make sure that you combine learning and counseling in an interactive activity.

Real-World Applications

Observational Extensions

Observe children on the playground. Are all of the children included in the group? Are some children being left out? Observe a group of teenagers talking. Is everyone included in the discussion? Do one or two teenagers do most of the talking? How can you make sure that these two situations do not happen in your after-school program?

Troubleshooting Checklists for Organizing a New After-School Program

1. Do your intervention strategies lead to cohesion?
2. How are you minimizing the disruptions to interaction?
3. Are you making sure that every single student is involved?

A Ready-to-Use Group-Centered Learning Center Intervention, Designing a Learning Center for Generating Interaction: Giving to Others

Even if you do not have access to a kitchen, your students can enjoy making bread dough faces. Children and teens will talk and interact while they make bread dough faces. Having the students make gifts for others also helps to generate altruistic group building. You may either make the bread dough in advance and have it ready for the students to use or have the students read the recipe and make the bread dough as well as the faces. For young children, I strongly suggest making the bread dough in advance or using a machine for kneading.

Recipe

5 cups of flour
2 teaspoons of salt
½ cup of sugar
3 packets of quick rise yeast
3 eggs
½ cup of margarine
½ cup of milk
½ cup of water

Have raisins, candied cherries, or other eatable items for making smiley faces.

Heat margarine milk and water until the margarine melts or liquid comes to a slight boil. Mix dry ingredients together. Add warm milk–margarine mixture to dry ingredients. Use a food processor with a bread dough hook or knead by hand. Knead until dough is thoroughly mixed, smooth, and ready to work by hand. Have greased baking sheets on hand for bread dough faces. Heat oven to 300°. Bread dough faces will be slightly brown around the edges when they are done. It is difficult to give an exact time because it depends on how much dough the students use when making the faces and hair.

GIVING TO OTHERS

Step 1: Our focus today will be on giving to others rather than on making a project for ourselves. We're going to make bread dough faces. We will take bread dough and shape it into a face with hair. You may be as creative as you want, but your face will only have two eyes, one nose, and one mouth. We also want to make nice faces, not ugly faces or monsters. You will make two happy faces. One face will go to the hunger center's silent auction to raise money for hungry children here in our community. And yes, it is difficult to believe that there are children living here in our community who do not have enough food to eat, but unfortunately, it is true. The second bread dough face that you make will be shared during snack time with a member of our group.

Step 2: Our first job is to wash our hands and arms with soap—all the way to our elbows. Make sure that your hands are dry before you start on the bread dough. Remember, when we work with food that we never rub our clean hands on our clothes or on our mouth or nose. If your hands get dirty, wash them again before touching food.

Step 3: The workstation helper will give each person a clump of bread dough—about the size of a billiard ball. Remember, bread dough has yeast in it and that yeast makes the bread rise; so your bread face is going to get larger.

Step 4: Roll the bread dough in your hands to make a round, smooth ball. Then, press the round ball flat with the palm of your hand on to a greased baking sheet.

Step 5: Place two raisins for eyes and half of a candied cherry for a mouth. Press these into the bread dough circle. Use a tiny bit of dough for the nose. Roll dough between your fingers until it is round. Then, gently put in place on the bread dough face.

Step 6: For hair, your workstation helper will give you a second clump of bread dough. This time you must be creative. Do you want spikey hair, braids, or hair that simply molds to the top of the head? Make your bread dough face look nice.

Step 7: Once you have finished your first bread dough face, repeat the process and make a second face to share with a friend from our group.

ARE YOU READY FOR A CHALLENGE?

Challenge Step: If interested, wash and dry your hands. Then, write a story about the face you have created. Give your face a name and create a nice adventure for your bread dough face.

Chapter 7
Solving Conflicts and Problems

She was an 11-year-old third grader who had been placed in the school district's alternative school for fighting. Her reading score was below the first grade level. She walked into the room looking for a fight. She was loud and pushy. She constantly tried to make herself the center of attention. Large for her age, she was almost as tall as me. During the first 2 months, she managed to get into trouble every single session, sometimes as she walked in the door. One day, a small second-grade student who lived in her neighborhood made a comment to her. He took off running (which of course was not allowed), and she took off after him. I stepped between them and yelled very loudly, "Stop! Sit! Right now!" We stood nose to nose with her glaring at me. I repeated my command, "Sit down! Now!" She finally gave in, yanked a chair out, and dropped into it. I had my assistant immediately clear the classroom; I sent the other students to continue working at other learning centers in other rooms. The little boy was sent to sit in the hallway to wait until I was able to talk with him. My main objective was to separate the two students immediately. I talked with each student individually. They were each assigned a dictionary page to sit and copy and sent to separate unused classrooms to work. At the end of the day's session before they left to go home, I talked with the two students together. I had each student tell me how they should have handled the situation, and then I asked each student to tell me what they should have done to prevent the situation from occurring in the first place. Last but not least, I had each student tell me how they planned to behave at the next session.

I told each student that I liked them both very much and enjoyed having them in my program but that I would not tolerate such behavior at the Reading Orienteering Club. I stated every behavior that was unacceptable—making rude comments about others, running, threatening .... I told both students that I looked forward to seeing them at our next session, and that I expected both of them to behave appropriately. Fortunately, at the next session, things were better. Both students began to settle down and work. No, their behavior was not perfect, and there were still minor incidents. By the end of the year, the 11-year-old girl had moved up two grade levels in reading and the little boy was ready to start third grade.

E. Clanton Harpine, *After-School Prevention Programs for At-Risk Students:* *Promoting Engagement and Academic Success*, DOI 10.1007/978-1-4614-7416-6_7, © Springer Science+Business Media New York 2013

The girl returned for a second year, since her reading score was still below her age level; unfortunately, the little boy's grandmother, with whom he lived, moved away, so I do not know what progress he made. In her second year, the girl returned to my program with a school suspension for fighting. On the first day, she arrived with her old attitude. I took her aside and reminded her that such behavior was not acceptable at the Reading Orienteering Club and that we had ended the year last year cooperating and working together very nicely. I told her that I was very happy to have her back and looked forward to working with her another year. From that point on, when she would start to get in trouble, I would simply call her name and say, "you know that is unacceptable; let's get to work; we have work to do." And yes, my children know what the word unacceptable means. I'm very happy to report that the student rarely ever gets in trouble anymore, is one of my hardest workers, and is continuing to make excellent progress in reading.

If you work with children or teenagers in an after-school program, you know that conflicts and problems will arise. The question that remains is how can you best deal with these conflicts and problems and still retain the group-centered cohesive structure that you are trying to develop for your after-school program. I have worked with children and teenagers in group programs for 41 years, and I will be the first to tell you that I do not have all of the answers. I've had the privilege of working with children from many different settings. I mostly work with at-risk populations. I've worked with children in the projects in Chicago, children from the Bronx, children who have been expelled from the public school system in Tampa, inner-city community and school groups in Ohio and Georgia, Hispanic immigrant populations in Texas, and children from rural poor neighborhoods in South Carolina. No matter where I have traveled and worked, there have always been children in need. When children are in need, there is conflict. In this chapter, we analyze several different examples and how these examples might relate to your own work. My goal is to help you think about problems before they arise so that you can be prepared and respond in the best way possible.

Violence Teaches Violence

I oppose any form of physical or corporal punishment with children or teenagers. Spanking is wrong. Any form of spanking simply models violence and demonstrates to young people that the only way to settle your problems is through violence. Research tells us that corporal punishment (any form of spanking, even a simple swat with a flat hand) increases violence and aggression and reduces academic improvement (Gershoff 2010). Yet, over half of the toddlers in the United States and 60 % of elementary students are spanked (Gershoff 2010). Although I do not believe in physical punishment, I do believe that children should be taught that there are consequences to your actions and that you are responsible for how you treat others. I advocate positive group experiences, but I do not advocate ignoring misbehavior.

Changing Behavior

Behavioral change requires more than just positive feelings. Behavioral change requires that students change how they think. Children are not born with bad behavior. Children learn inappropriate behavior through peer groups, dysfunctional families, and harsh neighborhoods, and from teasing, bullying, or belittling experiences with others (Criss et al. 2002). Much of a child's negative thinking begins before the child is even a year old. How often do you hear someone say, "You're a bad boy or you're a bad girl." Without thinking of the consequences, we often tell small children that they are bad. Actually, it is not the child who is bad; it is the behavior that is unacceptable. You should never tell a young child or any child or any teenager: "You're bad," because when you do, you are contributing to a negative self-image. When children arrive at your after-school program, they enter with a history of positive and negative experiences, a personality, a self-concept, high or low self-efficacy, and positive or negative self-esteem. Self-esteem, self-concept, and self-efficacy are all components of personality, and if we want to talk about changing student behavior, we must understand the interrelationship of these different variables.

We have discussed self-efficacy and self-esteem in previous chapters. Self-esteem is how I feel about myself, but a positive self-esteem does not necessarily lead to positive, desirable behavior (Baumeister et al. 2003). I may even be very proud of myself for starting a fight, but that does not mean that starting a fight is a positive behavior that I should strive for. Self-efficacy is my belief that I can accomplish a task. Rebuilding self-efficacy can contribute to behavioral change. A teenager with whom I worked for several years, who failed in reading for nine straight years, had a lengthy behavioral record and constantly got into trouble at school. Once the student learned to read, the behavioral problems vanished, but, as illustrated by our opening example, rebuilding self-efficacy and improved academic performance do not always correct behavioral problems. Sometimes, it takes more than just rebuilding self-efficacy to change behavior.

Create a Positive Cohesive Group Environment

I am not trying to say that a positive group, in and of itself, will change behavior any more than positive self-esteem corrects behavioral problems. This is why many attempts at the so-called positive discipline fail. For example, a little boy was sent to the principal's office one day for getting in trouble in class at a school which advocated "positive discipline." The principal talked to the little boy, and then sent him back to class with a sparkly pencil. What did the little boy and the rest of the class learn? If you want a sparkly pencil, get in trouble.

Behavioral change does require a positive atmosphere, but we cannot simply tack the word positive onto our discipline programs and then expect success. Cohesion is necessary before change can occur (Marmarosh et al. 2005). Students who misbehave in a group must feel accepted by others in the group before they will ever attempt to change their behavior. In essence, if I do not like a group, then I may not care whether I treat people nicely or not. For cohesion to develop in a group, there needs to be genuine caring and acceptance of others and the ideas and feelings of others. There also needs to be a change in self-image. It seems that it's always easier to misbehave than it is to behave, that it's easier to join a group in teasing rather than not join in teasing, or that it's easier to get angry than it is to stay calm when we feel that someone has mistreated us.

Self-concept is the knowledge, information, or definition I have in my own mind of who I am (Baumeister 1997). Self-concept requires that I think about my abilities, my body image, and my attitudes, and includes the values and moral structures that I have been taught. Self-concept is more complex than self-esteem and involves more than just positive feelings (Baumeister et al. 1989). Self-concept requires reflection; self-esteem does not. To change behavior, I must change not only what I think, but how I act and react to the world around me. The way in which a child or a teenager views a situation may be totally different than the way in which the adult views what is happening. If we want children and teenagers to adopt our standards of right and wrong, our principles of good behavior versus improper behavior, then we must create a group, a cohesive group which demonstrates and models the desired behavior. We must also teach young people to analyze their behavior and teach them how to make wise decisions. Good behavior does not automatically happen when a student joins a well-designed after-school program.

Appropriate Behavior Must Be Taught

I believe that if your after-school program is to be truly successful, you must have a structure that encourages children and teens to change. In real life, there are consequences to our actions; therefore, your program should also incorporate consequences to improper actions. As I often tell my students, "When I'm driving, I must follow the rules of the road. I cannot simply drive through a red light or stop sign if I do not feel like obeying the rules. By not following such rules, I would cause accidents, hurt others, and possibly even myself. Actions have consequences. The same is true in our group. I cannot simply act however I wish or say whatever I feel like saying to someone else. I must think before I act. I must think before I speak. I must consider how my actions and my words will affect others."

This is what I mean by developing a cohesive group atmosphere. Your students must care about each other. They must care whether they hurt someone else's feelings or not. Until they do, you will not change behavior.

A Potential Fight

In 41 years of working with children and teenagers in group situations, including inner-city settings, I have never had an actual fight take place in any of my groups. I have had several potential fight situations arise, but I've always been able to diffuse the hostilities. Perhaps I have been simply lucky, but I feel that this is also due to my approach to handling potentially explosive situations.

Let's begin by examining the example with which I introduced this chapter. Obviously an ill-mannered remark or unkind word sparked anger and a desire to retaliate. It is always better to stop a fight with words, if possible, rather than to pull two students apart. In a fight situation, if at all possible, I try never to physically touch either student involved. I use short, firm, loud commands: Stop! Sit! Now! In the heat of the moment, I never try to explain that such behavior is inappropriate. My goal is simply to separate the students and calm the situation. We must also remember that children are irrational and pumping with adrenaline when they switch into fight mode; therefore, long sentences or complicated explanations will not be heard. Use short quick commands. And, actually, I agree with many public school teachers, a fight between two teenage girls can be harder to stop than a fight between two teenage boys. I use the same strategies with teenagers as those I use with defusing fights between children.

Obviously, your goal is to prevent fights from developing, but, in all honesty, you need to know in advance how you will handle a fight situation. If you are working with at-risk students, the air is always ripe for a fight to develop. Children and teens who come from at-risk communities often come from family and neighborhood situations where disagreements and arguments are settled through fights or violence. Many at-risk students settle disagreements at school by fighting; therefore, when students first arrive at your program, they assume that the way to solve a problem is to fight. It is up to you to teach them other alternatives.

For instance, the young lady mentioned in our opening situation is now in her second year in my after-school program. She still has anger management problems, but I'm trying to teach her alternatives to fighting. One alternative that is working very well has been to teach her to pick up a book and sit down and read when she is frustrated or angry. This lets her calm down. Naturally, this did not work when she first joined the group. I first had to teach her how to read and then teach her to enjoy reading before I could teach her to use reading as an anger management tool. Now, if she becomes upset or is about to get in trouble, I will suggest that she go to the reading room and sit and read quietly for a few minutes. Our reading room is a small library with floor pillows and stuffed animals. The children enjoy plopping down on a pillow with a stuffed animal to read. It's very comforting and, in this case, gives our young student a chance to calm down without punishment. I'm careful not to let it become a habit or a way to get out of work, but it is an alternative that is working very well with this student.

This same student participates in another community program. That program gives the children candy (extrinsic reward) when they behave or do as they are told. The young lady from my opening example is often in trouble for fighting there. She behaves when she wants the candy, but candy is not a strong enough incentive to keep her from fighting. Candy has also not taught her to change her behavior. As mentioned earlier, candy is an extrinsic motivator; it teaches compliance but not change.

I do not agree with those who contend that timeout or sitting and copying a dictionary page will harm a child's self-esteem or that such is harmful to development. No one likes to use a dictionary. I have a dictionary sitting on my desk right now as I write, but it's not because I like dictionaries. Therefore, I do not fall for the claim that I will teach children to hate dictionaries because they copy dictionary pages when they misbehave. Verbal warnings or motivational incentives are my preferred method for maintaining order. My assistant and I are constantly rotating between the classrooms throughout the entire 2-hour program, so we know what is taking place in each room. If I see a problem arising, I frequently will say, "Come on, let's get to work; we have a TV show to produce today. We need puppeteers and puppets; who is going to be ready to read for our show today?" Whenever possible, it is always better to diffuse a problem before it becomes a problem.

The children in my *Reading Orienteering Club* program know that when they are told to sit and copy a dictionary page they have acted in a way that is inappropriate for our program. Copying a page from the dictionary allows the student to calm down so that we can discuss their behavior. I never try to explain rational behavior to a student while they are still angry. A period of calm reflection is good for all of us.

For the first 2 months in my *Reading Orienteering Club* after-school program, I am always on the alert for potential arguments and fights. I work with a very at-risk population. I work with children who come from drug-infested neighborhoods and dysfunctional homes, and sometimes with children who do not have homes. By the third or fourth month in my program, I rarely worry about any of my students trying to fight, even if they are angry. Why? I stress the development of the group, the building of cohesion, and that we are a team and we work together, but I will admit, the first 2 months with a new at-risk population can be very difficult. Never give up. The principles that I teach work, and I use them each and every day.

Be prepared. Know how you will respond if a fight does occur, and remember to teach the students that actions have consequences. No, I do not simply send my students home if they get in trouble. I feel that students must learn to work through their problems, including their dislike of other group members. There are consequences for misbehavior, but never rewards for good behavior. Good behavior is the expected norm, not something to be rewarded.

Although fights are one of the biggest concerns, they are by no means the only conflicts that arise. It is sometimes the behavior that instigates the fight that is the hardest to control.

Teasing, Bullying, and Belittling

Academic failure is not the only way in which children and teens feel ostracized. One of our biggest problems in neighborhoods, schools, and even in some families is that children and teens are often made to feel inferior in groups and among their peers by how others talk to them and act toward them. The little boy mentioned in the opening example came from a very dysfunctional family. He seemed very shy and quiet. Upon first meeting him, you would think that he rarely talked. Actually, he would slip around and very quietly make rude comments to other children, usually children who were larger and older than he is. Then, he would take off running. I never saw him tease or make fun of anyone younger. In an after-school program, it is not our job to explore why this little boy was picking on students who were older and larger than himself. Obviously, at some point in his life, he was teased and belittled. His response was to get others in trouble. At first glance, no one would have expected him to be the one initiating the fights and conflicts; yet, children bring many problems and problem behaviors to your after-school program. You must teach your students new ways of behaving in a peer group setting. As I often tell my students, "No matter how you act at home, at school, or in your neighborhood, when you come to the *Reading Orienteering Club* I expect for you to remember that we are a team and we work together. Everyone is accepted on our team, and we absolutely never make fun of, laugh at, tease, say rude words to, or hurt anyone's feelings. We're here to work, so let's get to work and help each other."

I do not have a long list of rules that I post up on the wall or read off to the children, but I do remind the children when friction arises of our team concept and that we always work together. I also make sure that the students realize that my expectations and rules at the after-school program are not the same as those at school or at home. I work from a counseling base, which is not the same as in a school classroom structure; therefore, I remind the students that at the *Reading Orienteering Club* I expect different behavior from what they may normally display at home or at school. As the group develops, behavioral expectations develop as well. This is where the 11 therapeutic factors discussed earlier become very important in the development of your group. These factors will help you bring about the behavioral change that you want to achieve. Refer back to Chap. 3 and review these therapeutic factors if needed. Make sure that you are incorporating the 11 therapeutic factors into your learning center workstations. They are your steps to behavioral change.

When to Use Designated Groups

In Chap. 6, we discussed the importance of keeping the learning centers interactive. It is important to allow students to move freely from learning center to learning center at their own pace. This individualizes instruction, challenges those who are ready to move ahead, and provides an opportunity for those who need extra help in a particular area to seek that help. This concept works very well and I have used it for many years. The only problem is if you have a group of students who clump together and cause problems. Somehow, those who want to cause trouble always seem to cluster around others who desire to cause trouble. If it is a minor situation, you can simply start trouble-prone students at different learning center workstations. This often gives you the distribution and dispersion that you seek, thereby reducing the likelihood for problems to arise. Nevertheless, if trouble persists, another method that I have successfully used is to form designated groups on the basis of behavior problems, or in other words, to put all of my troublemakers in one group. Let's look at an example.

I had a group of 12 first- and second-grade boys who were constantly getting in trouble. They were not fighting, but they were also not working. This was the first few weeks of a new year-long program, and I wanted to impress upon these young gentlemen the necessity of working. None of the 12 could read, so they definitely needed to be involved in the program. I had spoken to them several times about getting their work done, but they were more interested in having a good time. At the start of a session, I pulled them together in one group. Then, I sent the rest of the children off to the learning centers as usual. I took my special group of 12 to a separate room with only chalkboard and flash cards. I began to drill them on the vowel cluster material being covered at the learning centers.

Every time someone smarted off, we stopped our work and discussed appropriate group behavior, not a lecture but more as a counseling group. I asked questions. Why did you say that? Do you think that helps or hurts us learn to read? Why do you feel you need to act that way? How can you change the way you act in a group? How could you have responded differently? I did this for several sessions. This group of 12 did not make hands-on projects, did not work at the learning center stations, or participate in the TV show for this special designated session. They just worked in my designated group with flash cards and the chalkboard. We did word games which they enjoyed, but they still knew that they were missing out on the rest of the program. Finally, one little boy ask, "Will we ever get to go back and work like the others?" I explained that when they could show me they could go back and work nicely at the learning center workstations, I would be happy to have them do so. At the next session, they returned to the workstations. I had to give a few reminders that we were here to work, but the boys settled down. It was not necessary for me to repeat a designated group to control their behavior.

The point that I exemplified and explained to the boys was that we were going to do the work. We could do it the fun way, or we could do it the hard way. It was their choice.

Any time you use designated groups, you break up the flow and development of interaction which leads to a cohesive group, but sometimes, it is necessary. As long as misbehavior continued, I was not achieving my goal for a cohesive group. I needed to restructure. I allowed those students who were working correctly to continue. I pulled my mischievous group aside to work with them separately so that I did not disrupt the group process with the other students.

It is very important that when you discipline students in a group that you only discipline those who are misbehaving. Always pull misbehaving students aside. Allow other students to continue. The worst classroom tactic ever developed is for a teacher to penalize an entire class because of the actions of a few. Do not make this same mistake. In your after-school program, keep the atmosphere positive; take misbehaving students aside and work with them individually or in a designated group. Then, praise your entire group when they come back together and work the way you want them to.

Refusal to Work

It is rare in my program for a student not to become excited by all of the hands-on projects. At the end of the year, when asked what did you like best about the program, students inevitably say the projects. At each session, the students work on a different hands-on project, but remember, each project is linked to teaching vowel clusters and capturing words. Although children do not get tired of hands-on projects, they do get tired of vowels and learning new vowel clusters. Sometimes children will say, "I just want to make a rocket; I don't want to do all that word junk." I always smile and explain, "You can't have one without the other. We're here to work, and one of our jobs is to practice vowel sounds. We're just using the rocket to help us practice."

I make sure that my program has a fun atmosphere. I want the children to enjoy coming to the *Reading Orienteering Club*. As I tell the children, "I want you to love reading and learn how much fun reading can be." At the same time, I want the children to realize that our purpose is not just to play. It is my job to teach them a new way to learn how to read, to teach them that they can succeed where they have failed in the past, to teach them a new way to behave and act toward others in a group, and to teach them to be proud of themselves for real accomplishments—to rebuild their self-efficacy.

Make your program fun and enjoyable, but keep your focus on learning and change. Never let your hands-on projects become purely craft projects. Just as my *Reading Orienteering Club* is so much more than merely a reading program, my hands-on intrinsic motivators are so much more than simple craft projects; they are teaching tools. So this is why when a parent said, "My son has to leave early today and we won't be able to be at the next session; so can he just finish his race car before we leave? He really likes the little car and wants to finish it." My response was, "No, but I'll be glad to keep his car and he can finish when he returns." I went on to explain that our purpose was not to just make a car (although the car did have wheels that turned, vowel-clustered racing stripes, and an exhaust pipe that spewed captured words); I explained that the car's purpose was to help the children practice vowel sounds and captured words. The little boy left without his car, and the parent was most upset with me. Don't give in. If you ever allow hands-on projects to become a paper-glue craft project, you have sacrificed their value as an intrinsic motivator and teaching tool.

Parents

It may seem strange to discuss parents in a chapter about conflicts. I assure you that parents can be one of your greatest assets or biggest hindrances. I have parents who still seek me out several years after their child was in my program to tell me how grateful they are and how much their child has changed or how well the child is doing in school. I have parents who come after work each week for our make-believe TV shows and stand exhausted and tired in greasy, grimy work clothes, glowing with pride as they listen to their children read. I also have a parent in my program who volunteers and directs snack time every single session. She makes sure that we have snacks and that they are healthy snacks. She also oversees our snack period, making sure that every student is ready to go to work on time. Unfortunately, not every parent is so dedicated and helpful.

Some parents only want an after-school program to babysit their children and help their children finish their homework. If you try to make your after-school program more than just a place to do homework, then you will have conflict with some parents. As one parent explained to me, "I need you to get his homework done, so I don't have to bother." If you are developing a reteaching program as I have done with *vowel clustering* and the *4-step method* for teaching at-risk students to read, then you may encounter parents who do not understand the kind of program that you are offering. As one parent stated, "He's been in your program for 2 weeks. Why can't he read?" We know from research that it takes over 100 hours of intensive retraining to help children who are failing in reading to be able to undo such failure and begin to learn again (Keller and Just 2009). For some students, it takes more than 100 hours. Intensive skills training can help students (Meyler et al. 2008), but it is sometimes hard to explain to parents, who may themselves not be able to read, that you are trying to reorganize the connectivity and organization of fibers within the brain (Draganski et al. 2006) so that their children will be able to read and succeed in school. Many parents do not understand why retraining is so complicated and time-consuming. They want immediate results.

My only advice is to continue to restate the importance of what you are doing and why your program is organized and conducted as it is. Explain your objectives and report the progress your students are making. Progress reports do help with parents. Also, do not give in. Do not become a homework station just to please parents. Yes, some parents will pull their children out of your program if you do not cater to their homework demands. I had one mother take her son and his cousin out of my program because I refused to help them work on their homework. We should remind ourselves at this point that research has shown that homework does not improve academic progress or grades (Cooper et al. 2006). Both boys were doing very well in my after-school program and wanted to continue. My program only meets for 2 hours 2 days a week. There is an hour and a half gap between the time that school is dismissed and when my program begins. When I suggested that she was welcome to sit down and help her children do their homework before our session started, as some other parents did, she informed me that she was much too busy, had other children, and that I should help her children complete their homework before they started on what I had planned for the day. Yes, some parents are a blessing, while others will never understand what you are trying to do.

Although most of our attention in this chapter has been on what to do when trouble occurs, our design section will look at how we might keep some of these problems from arising. No, nothing is foolproof, but the more you aim for success, the more likely you are to achieve success. We will look at three aspects of change.

Although we have talked about these three aspects earlier, in this chapter, we talk about them in reference to controlling and changing behavior. Again, I will offer examples from my *Reading Orienteering Club* program.

Step 7: Designing a Learning Center to Change Behavior

What is the most important component of your program which will help you achieve behavioral change?

How will you encourage students to work together nicely in a group?

What aspects of your program will challenge students to change how they interact with others in a group setting?

Step 7, Design Example

Most important component of change. Rebuilding self-efficacy is your first step in motivating students to change their behavior. If I perceive myself to be a failure, I am not likely to care how I treat others. Anger and ostracism may even lead a student to strike out at others, so your first step toward change is to demonstrate to students that they are not failures by teaching them the skills that they need to perform successfully academically. In my program, I teach reading. I start rebuilding self-efficacy on the very first day; *vowel clustering* allows students to begin to read simple vowel-clustered stories the first day of the program. For a student, who has always failed in reading or has never been able to read a story before, reading even a simple vowel-clustered story is very exciting. From day one, the student begins to believe that there just might be *hope* and that they just might be able to learn to read. By instilling *hope* in my students, they become more willing to listen and work with me. I start off very slowly with *The Story of At.* Next, *Andy the Ant,* again a very simple vowel-clustered story, allows beginning students to read. (To remind yourself how to write a vowel-clustered story, return to *The Hat Cat* in Chap. 1.) Step by step, skill by skill, I teach students to read. As explained earlier in the chapter, sometimes excitement over learning is enough to change behavior patterns, and sometimes it is not. Either way, rebuilding self-efficacy is my foundation and my first step toward behavioral change.

Encouraging polite, constructive behavior. The group process that surrounds my hands-on learning center workstations is my element for change which encourages polite, constructive behavior. Yes, the children want to make the hands-on craft projects. To make the project, they must work together in small groups at the workstations. Remember that hands-on craft projects supply intrinsic motivation and serve as a teaching tool for *vowel clustering* and *capturing tricky words*, and building the hands-on projects generates constructive interaction and polite behavior. The students are only allowed to complete the hands-on project if they are working politely with others; therefore, polite behavior is continuously being *modeled* as the children travel from workstation to workstation. When a student does not model polite behavior, the student is removed from the workstation. Therefore, over and over the students are taught that it is polite behavior that enables you to work at the workstations. It is very important that the hands-on projects never become an extrinsic reward, for that would diminish their value; every student must be included and must be helped to make the hands-on project, unless they force their removal from the workstation by their improper behavior. What I'm saying is, never use the hands-on projects as a reward: "If you behave, I'll let you make ...." If a student must be removed from a workstation, students are then allowed to return to the work that is being done at the workstation. They are allowed to read the vowel-clustered stories. They are allowed to capture the words, but students are never allowed to just make a project or take home a partially finished project—even if they behave. To finish a project, the student must complete the reading work that is attached to that project, and good behavior only gives the student the opportunity to work.

Challenging students to change their behavior and how they interact with others. My interactive projects (puppet plays, painting, and the TV studio) continuously challenge my students to change their behavior. To be in a puppet play, they must cooperate. Students are never allowed to tease, laugh at, or make fun of someone else while working in a small group to present a puppet play. The TV studio concept also helps. I often tell students, "you cannot go on the TV news acting rude and obnoxious (I do not include reality television.)." Even my youngest students or my most frequently misbehaving students comprehend the difference between presenting the news (as shown on real TV) and making a fool of yourself (as displayed by many reality TV shows), or as one student said, "I like to watch it [reality TV], but I sure wouldn't want someone filming me doing that." Even my most difficult students seem to know how they are supposed to behave; the task is getting them to do it. Build exciting interactive projects into your program, and such projects will help.

Real-World Applications

Observational Extensions

Go to a playground or park and watch children or teens argue. Hopefully the argument will not escalate into an actual fight. Observe what is happening when the argument begins. Observe nonverbal behavior during the argument. Look at the situation: How could the argument have been prevented? Can you apply any of these ideas to your own group?

Troubleshooting Checklists for Organizing a New After-School Program

1. Do you have a plan or a procedure in your after-school program in case a fight does occur? Is your staff (including volunteers) well versed on this plan? Make sure that everyone knows how to handle a potential fight situation and what staff members are expected to do.
2. Do your students face consequences for improper actions or words? What kind of consequences do you use? Do such consequences take away your desire to build a cohesive group structure?
3. Do you have a plan for talking with parents and explaining your program and its objectives to parents?
4. How will you handle students who do not wish to participate in your program?
5. What will you say to students who are disruptive?

A Ready-to-Use Group-Centered Learning Center Intervention, Designing a Learning Center for Changing Behavior: Painting Pictures in the Clouds

When I need to teach control with a group, I frequently use a creative art painting project. Children and teens love to paint. At-risk students rarely have an opportunity to paint; therefore, they are more eager to listen and comply with rules for an opportunity to paint. You never want painting to become an extrinsic reward—"If you behave, I will let you paint." Make sure that painting is one of your designated workstations and that everyone is given an opportunity to paint. If you are forced to use designated groups as a means of developing group cooperation and encouraging students to work, then a structured creative art painting session, such as the one I describe in this example, can be an excellent approach for teaching group members how to work together. This learning center example works with ADHD children and teens who struggle with impulsivity, for children and teens working on anger management, and for children and teens who wrestle to control bullying and bossy behavior toward others. This workstation works best in groups of ten, unless you have teenagers prone to fight: then I suggest groups of five. I always announce that we are doing a group painting project today, everyone will receive a turn, but we will work in groups of ten. You may assign groups for this project and simply have students work at the other learning centers until their group is called. Everyone gets a turn, but I always call on the most cooperative people first. Since I'm teaching cooperation, this does not take away from my group goals as long as I make sure that every single student gets a turn to paint. Even my rowdiest students settle down for a turn to paint. It will take some students a little longer than others to grasp the idea, but painting has a way of encouraging compliance.

In my program, group paintings are used to make cloth puppet stages. We paint ocean scenes, cabins in the woods, spring flowers, galaxies, and, for the project as described in this example, scenes from books we have read. Painting a cloth puppet stage must be stretched over several sessions in order for the paint to dry and not smear as each new layer is added. The instructions given in this example are for only one day and only one workstation. There is not room in this book to present the entire project. In the example that I present below, the children have already painted a blue sky, green grass, a small duck pond, and a large tree. These items could easily be painted in designated groups as well and are all dry and ready to have the finishing touches added. As always in group paintings, I have my students paint from left to right so that we do not smear the painting of others as new groups come to paint. For puppet stages, I simply use an old bed sheet. Cloth takes paint as well as paper and is much more durable. I put a plastic drop cloth down to minimize cleanup, stretch the bedsheet down on top of the plastic, and then give the children the instructions I want them to follow. I want my painting sessions to be creative, fun, lively, but instructional. I absolutely always have a workstation helper at my painting table. I have a collection of simple (easy-to-read) books about the weather and clouds. Check the children's section in the library if you do not have access to easy reading books about clouds. This project actually includes three stories which introduce the objects being painted: (1) a story about clouds, (2) a story about apples in an orchard—the children paint thumbprint apples on the tree, and (3) a story about ducks swimming in a pond—the children use their thumb and little fingertip to make a duck each in our duck pond. Each story is done separately so that the paint may dry.

PAINTING PICTURES IN THE CLOUDS

Step 1: We are painting as a group today. Everyone will get a turn, but we must wait patiently and paint one at a time so that we do not smear someone else's painting. Put on a painting shirt, find a chair, and wait until you are called to paint. We will read a story, and then paint something from the story. Let's listen to our story. Who would like to read nice and loud so that we can all hear?

Step 2: Story:

Clouds

On a warm summer day, I like to go cloud watching.

First, I need clouds.

Second, I find a nice grassy spot where I can stretch out and stare at the sky.

Then, I simply let my imagination go to work.

I look for animal shapes in the clouds.

There's a cat, a caterpillar, and that cloud could even be a horse.

What do you see when you look at the clouds?

Step 3: Did you like the story about pretending to see shapes in the clouds? Have you ever been outside, looked at the sky, and pretended that a cloud was an animal or some other kind of shape? Well, we're going to do exactly that, except we're going to paint our shapes. Are you ready? We are going to paint clouds. Not just round circles, but animal shapes just like in the story. If you cannot think of an animal that you want to paint, think back to the story. A caterpillar can be made with three or four circles. A cat or a dog can be made from two circles with ears and a tail. A mouse or a whale can be made from one single circle. Use your imagination. Be creative and think while you're waiting for a turn.

Step 4: We are only using white paint today because clouds are white, but by varying the amount of paint you use, it's possible to give your cloud a whispery affect. Our goal today is not to demonstrate our skill in painting, but to show that we can work together as a group and make a nice group painting that we will be proud to use for our puppet stage.

Step 5: Remember that we always paint from left to right and that we keep our pictures small enough so that everyone will be able to find blue sky on which to paint their cloud. So think before you paint. We also do not want our cloud pictures to be so squished together that we cannot tell what the cloud represents. Remember we absolutely never paint over or damage someone else's work. We will start on the left-hand side and work across the sky so that there will always be a space for others to paint when they come to the station. We always want to think of the needs of others, not just what we want. Think before you paint. You may even want to take a pencil and paper and draw the animal or shape that you would like to turn into a cloud. Make sure that you put on a paint cover up shirt before you start. Use the white paint and go slow. We want nice neat cloud shapes. Paint one cloud, and then wash your hands and go to the challenge step or to the next station. Remember, others are waiting for their turn.

ARE YOU READY FOR A CHALLENGE?

Challenge Step: Take a piece of blue construction paper and paint your cloud shape on the blue paper. Write your name in the corner. Next, use a piece of writing paper and write a story about your cloud. I hope you will read your story to us at the end of our session today. Be creative.

Chapter 8
After-School Programs and the School Mission

He was 18 years old and had just been ushered into my first-grade reading program. He was one of 30 children who had been thrown out of the public school for severe behavioral problems. He was a member of a gang and very upset about being forced to participate in my program. He was on probation, and part of his court order insisted that he attend my community-based reading program. I normally do not divide groups by age, but in this case, I did. I placed 6- and 7-year-olds in one group, 8–11 in a second group, and 12–18 in my third group. I had worked in inner-city locations before, but I had just started my new reading program. I originally started out following in the footsteps of the schools by using reading groups; that idea was a total failure with students who had no desire to read. I introduced hands-on learning centers; the same teenagers who had no interest in reading became excited, except for my 18-year-old. He explained, "I don't need to read, I make good money, and the court just said I had to show up, didn't say I had to do nothing." I'm short, and he was over 6 ft tall. The likelihood of me being able to make him work was highly unlikely. Instead of arguing with him, I asked if he would be willing to help one of the other students. There was another teenager in the group who obviously had some developmental mental disorders. The two boys came from the same neighborhood, and I had noticed that he was somewhat protective of the other boy. He sat down and very slowly began to explain to the other teenager what he needed to do. They worked together, hour after hour, day after day. The program was only a summer intervention and not nearly long enough to bring about change with these students. Their problems were too severe for a short-term program, and the funding needed to extend the program was not available. Nonetheless, I have never forgotten how children and teens who had totally given up became excited about reading through hands-on learning centers. I also remember a very street-hardened 18-year-old who began to try learning to read so that he could help a friend.

"It is not enough to merely have good intentions," stated Dr. Keith Herman, keynote speaker, at the Second Annual School-Based Mental Health Group Interventions Conference; "our intentions must translate into actual help for those we seek to

E. Clanton Harpine, *After-School Prevention Programs for At-Risk Students: Promoting Engagement and Academic Success*, DOI 10.1007/978-1-4614-7416-6_8, © Springer Science+Business Media New York 2013

assist." Within this statement lies the heart of the problem confronting after-school programs. It has been our goal throughout this book to turn "good intentions" into successful results. We cannot just say that I would like to make my after-school program more successful; we must actually take steps to change after-school programming to make after-school programs successful (Granger 2010).

As pointed out in Chap. 1, merely buying an evidence-based program will not improve your after-school curriculum. The way in which a program is implemented can turn an evidence-based program from success to failure (McHugh and Barlow 2010). Therefore, in this book we have embarked upon the task of writing a new group-centered approach.

We have chosen a prevention focus for after-school programming because one of the primary goals of any prevention group is to bring about change and personal well-being (Clanton Harpine 2013b). For a prevention group to succeed, it must be interactive (Conyne and Clanton Harpine 2010). Constructive group interaction can lead to cohesion (Yalom and Leszcz 2005). Cohesion is essential if there is to be change (Marmarosh et al. 2005).

We have chosen a group-centered approach (Clanton Harpine 2008) for after-school programming because all group-centered programs must incorporate both learning and counseling (Clanton Harpine 2013a, b). A program cannot be classified as group centered if it does not include an emphasis on both learning and counseling (Clanton Harpine 2011a, b). This is important for after-school programs because learning and counseling cannot be separated, they are intertwined (Greenberg et al. 2003); this is important with a prevention-focused after-school program because prevention interventions will only succeed if they are interlinked with academic needs (Brigman and Webb 2007; Nation et al. 2003).

Using the group-centered approach, our after-school program must include rebuilding self-efficacy (Clanton Harpine 2011a, b). Rebuilding self-efficacy can only be accomplished through the teaching of skills (Bandura 1997). Yet, simply teaching academic skills does not fulfill the requirements of the group-centered approach. The group-centered approach also dictates that an after-school program must bring about interpersonal change as well as academic change. The 11 therapeutic factors (Yalom and Leszcz 2005) must be interwoven into any group-centered after-school program. This is best accomplished with hands-on learning centers that teach the academic skills needed to rebuild self-efficacy while offering group interactive interventions that lead to individual and group change (Clanton Harpine 2008). Being free to move between learning centers gives students a sense of independence, but learning centers also allow students to demonstrate control so that when they return to the classroom they have learned strategies to help them act appropriately (Klingberg et al. 2002). An effective after-school program for children or teenagers must include cognitive skills and intrinsic motivation in order to help students return to the classroom and demonstrate improvement (Pintrich and Schunk 2002). Such student improvement must not be limited to just the after-school program, but transfer back to the school classroom (Duckworth et al. 2007) and continue into change that lasts a lifetime (Obiakor 2001). The student's health and well-being rely on the healing power that groups can possess in order to bring about change in mental health (Salovey et al. 2000).

Groups have also been described as being the most logical prevention-oriented intervention and as providing the best ease of transference from the prevention program to real life (Kulic et al. 2004). Research shows that programs stressing change through group prevention lead to higher academic achievement, a lower dropout rate, reduced absenteeism and truancy, and fewer behavior problems. Rejection, teasing, bullying, and fighting are all reduced (Wandersman and Florin 2003). For an after-school prevention program to succeed, it must have a cohesive atmosphere (Wandersman et al. 2008). This is very important because children and youth have a need to belong, to be accepted by peers, to display a sense of personal accomplishment, and to develop a positive self-identify while maintaining a sense of control and pride over their personal life and actions (Suarez-Orozco and Suarez-Orozco 2001).

The group-centered approach encourages after-school programs to create a fun, hands-on learning environment. Keeping intrinsic motivation high is essential in a year-long program. Incorporating the therapeutic power of group process will help the students learn to problem-solve, test ideas, incorporate new ways of interacting together, and learn new positive behaviors. The group-centered approach also provides a structure in which students can learn how to resolve acceptance issues, coping with peer pressure, and how to handle teasing and bullying. The group-centered approach to after-school programming builds therapeutic group interventions into the learning center workstations so that all students who attend the program are offered the support and acceptance they need.

Your after-school program can help at-risk students rekindle the joy of learning and rebuild their self-efficacy but only if your program is successful. I spoke with the director of a local after-school program; some of the children from her program actually attend my twice-a-week *Reading Orienteering Club*; "how is it," she said "that the children learn to read and even behave when they come to you. In our program, no matter what we do, they refuse to read and they certainly don't behave." "You can accomplish just as much as I do," I replied, "but first, you must completely get rid of the program you're using and start over with a whole new approach—a group-centered approach."

Throughout the chapters of this book we have shown how to build a group-centered after-school prevention program. Step by step, the book provides the questions to help you apply the principles of the group-centered approach to your program and has also given design examples to show the depth of thinking and application that you should be applying to your design process. You are now ready to write your program. Return to chapters as needed to make sure that you have included each of the design principles. Remember that each step corresponds to the chapter and design principle it explains.

Step 1: Establish the focus of your program.

Step 2: Bring about academic improvement by rebuilding self-efficacy.

Step 3: Strive to enhance mental health and wellness by incorporating the 11 thera-
        peutic factors.

Step 4: Increase intrinsic motivation through hands-on activities.

Step 5: Generate change through the use of group-centered interventions.

Step 6: Encourage group interaction and cohesion.

Step 7: Control behavior.

Step 8: Write the final draft of your group-centered after-school prevention program
        and incorporate each of the group-centered principles.

References

Ablon, J., & Jones, E. (2002). Validity of controlled clinical trials of psychotherapy: Findings from the NIMH treatment of depression collaborative research program. *American Journal of Psychiatry, 159*, 775–783.

Adams, J. W., Snowling, M. J., Hennessy, S. M., & Kind, P. (1999). Problems of behavior, reading and arithmetic: Assessments of comorbidity using the strengths and difficulties questionnaire. *British Journal of Educational Psychology, 69*, 571–585.

Adelman, H. S., & Taylor, L. (2006). Mental health in schools and public health. *Public Health Report, 121*, 294–298.

Arnold, D. H., & Doctoroff, G. L. (2003). The early education of socio-economically disadvantaged children. *Annual Reviews in Psychology, 54*, 517–545.

Bandura, A. (1977). Self-efficacy: Toward a unifying theory of behavioral change. *Psychological Review, 84*, 191–215.

Bandura, A. (1986). *Social foundations of thought and action: A social cognitive theory.* Englewood Cliffs, NJ: Prentice-Hall.

Bandura, A. (1994). *Self-efficacy in changing societies.* New York: Cambridge University Press.

Bandura, A. (1995). Exercise of personal and collective efficacy in changing societies. In A. Bandura (Ed.), *Self-efficacy in changing societies* (pp. 1–45). New York: Cambridge University Press.

Bandura, A. (1997). *Self-efficacy: The exercise of control.* New York: W. H. Freeman.

Bandura, A. (1998). Health promotion from the perspective of social cognitive theory. *Psychological Health, 13*, 623–649.

Bandura, A., Barbaranelli, C., Vittorio Caprara, G., & Pastorelli, C. (2001). Self-efficacy beliefs as shapers of children's aspirations and career trajectories. *Child Development, 72*, 187–206.

Bandura, A., Blanchard, E., & Ritter, B. (1969). The relative efficacy of desensitization and modeling approaches for inducing behavioral, affective, and attitudinal changes. *Journal of Personality and Social Psychology, 13*, 173–199.

Bandura, A., & Schunk, D. H. (1981). Cultivating competence, self-efficacy, and intrinsic interest through proximal self-motivation. *Journal of Personality and Social Personality, 41*, 586–598.

Baumeister, R. F. (1997). Identity, self-concept, and self-esteem: The self lost and found. In R. Hogan, J. Johnson, & S. Briggs (Eds.), *Handbook of personality psychology* (pp. 681–711). New York: Academic Press.

Baumeister, R. F., Campbell, J. D., Krueger, J. I., & Vohs, K. D. (2003). Does high self-esteem cause better performance, interpersonal success, happiness, or healthier lifestyles? *Psychological Science in the Public Interest, 4*, 1–44.

E. Clanton Harpine, *After-School Prevention Programs for At-Risk Students:* *Promoting Engagement and Academic Success,* DOI 10.1007/978-1-4614-7416-6, © Springer Science+Business Media New York 2013

Baumeister, R. F., Campbell, J. D., Krueger, J. I., & Vohs, K. D. (2005). Exploding the self-esteem myth. *Scientific American, 292*, 84–92.

Baumeister, R. F., & Leary, M. (1995). The need to belong: Desire for interpersonal attachments as a fundamental human motivation. *Psychological Bulletin, 117*(3), 497–529.

Baumeister, R. F., Tice, D. M., & Hutton, D. G. (1989). Self-presentational motivations and personality differences in self-esteem. *Journal of Personality, 57*, 547–579.

Benware, C., & Deci, E. L. (1984). The quality of learning with an active versus passive motivational set. *American Educational Research Journal, 21*, 755–765.

Berking, M., Orth, U., Wupperman, P., Meier, L. L., & Caspar, F. (2008). Prospective effects of emotion-regulation skills on emotional adjustment. *Journal of Counseling Psychology, 55*, 485–494. doi:10.1037/a0013589.

Blaunstein, P., & Lyon, R. (2006). *Why kids can't read: Challenging the status quo in education*. Lanham, MD: Rowman and Littlefield Education.

Bradley, R. L. (2005). K-12 service-learning impacts: A review of state-level studies of service-learning. In J. Kielsmeier & M. Neal (Eds.), *Growing to Greatness 2005: The State of Service-Learning Project*. Saint Paul, MN: National Youth Leadership Council.

Brigman, G., & Webb, L. (2007). Student success skills: Impacting achievement through large and small group work. *Group Dynamics: Theory, Research, and Practice, 11*, 283–292. doi:10.1037/1089-2699.11.4.283.

Broderick, P. C., & Blewitt, P. (2006). *The life span: Human development for helping professionals* (2nd ed.). Upper Saddle River, NJ: Pearson.

Brody, G. H., Dorsey, S., Forehand, R., & Armistead, L. (2002). Unique and protective contributions of parenting and classroom processes to the adjustment of African American children living in single-parent families. *Child Development, 73*, 274–286.

Brook, J. S., Brook, D. W., De La Rosa, M., Whiteman, M., Johnson, E., & Montoya, I. (2001). Adolescent illegal drug use: The impact of personality, family, and environmental factors. *Journal of Behavioral Medicine, 24*, 183–203.

Brooks-Gunn, J. (2003). Do you believe in magic? What we can expect from early childhood intervention programs. *Social Policy Report: Giving Child and Youth Development Knowledge Away, 17*, 3–14.

Bryant, A., Schulenberg, J., O'Malley, P., Bachman, J., & Johnston, L. (2003). How academic achievement, attitudes, and behaviors relate to the course of substance use during adolescence: A 6-year, multinational longitudinal study. *Journal of Research on Adolescence, 13*, 361–397.

Bryck, R. L., & Fisher, P. A. (2012). Training the brain: Practical applications of neural plasticity from the intersection of cognitive neuroscience, developmental psychology, and prevention science. *American Psychologist, 67*, 87–100. doi:10.1037/a0024657.

Buhs, E. S., Ladd, G. W., & Herald, S. (2006). Peer exclusion and victimization: Processes that mediate the relation between peer group rejection and children's classroom engagement and achievement? *Journal of Educational Psychology, 98*, 1–13. doi:10.1037/0022-0663.98.1.1.

Cantor, N., Markus, H., Niedenthal, P., & Nurius, P. (1986). On motivation and the self-concept. In R. M. Sorrentino & T. Higgins (Eds.), *Handbook of motivation and cognition: Foundations of social behavior*. New York: The Guilford Press.

Castle, L., Aubert, R. E., Verbrugge, R. R., Khalid, M., & Epstein, R. S. (2007). Trends in medication treatment for ADHD. *Journal of Attention Disorders, 10*, 335–342.

Catalano, R. F., Mazza, J. J., Harachi, T. W., Abbott, R. D., Haggerty, K. P., & Fleming, C. B. (2003). Raising healthy children through enhancing social development in elementary school: Results after 1.5 years. *Journal of School Psychology, 41*, 143–164.

Chard, D. J., Vaughn, S., & Tyler, B. J. (2002). A synthesis of research on effective interventions for building reading fluency with elementary students with learning disabilities. *Journal of Learning Disabilities, 35*, 386–406.

Chessman, E. A., McGuire, J. M., Shankweiler, D., & Coyne, M. (2009). First-year teacher knowledge of phonemic awareness and its instruction. *Teacher Education and Special Education: The Journal of the Teacher Education Division of the Council for Exceptional Children, 32*, 270–289. doi:10.1177/0888406409339685.

Clanton Harpine, E. (2005, August). After-school community-based prevention project. In Carl Paternite (Chair), *Using community science to promote school-based mental health*. Symposium conducted at the annual convention of the American Psychological Association, Washington, DC.

Clanton Harpine, E. (2006, August). *Developing an effective cost-efficient after-school prevention program for community-based organizations*. Paper presented at the annual convention of the American Psychological Association, New Orleans, LA.

Clanton Harpine, E. (2007a, August). *A community-based after-school prevention program: A one year review of the Camp Sharigan program*. Paper presented at the annual convention of the American Psychological Association, San Francisco, CA.

Clanton Harpine, E. (2007b). Applying motivation theory to real-world problems. *Teaching of Psychology, 34*, 111–113.

Clanton Harpine, E. (2008). *Group interventions in schools: Promoting mental health for at-risk children and youth*. New York: Springer.

Clanton Harpine, E. (2010a). *Erasing failure in the classroom, vol. 1: Camp Sharigan, a ready-to-use group-centered intervention for grades 1–3* (2nd ed.). Aiken, SC: Group-Centered Learning.

Clanton Harpine, E. (2010b). *Erasing failure in the classroom, vol. 2: Vowel clustering, a ready-to-use classroom style group-centered intervention for teaching irregular vowel sounds to at-risk children and youth*. Aiken, SC: Group-Centered Learning.

Clanton Harpine, E. (2010c, August). *Developing a community literacy program: A university-community collaborative project*. Paper presented at the annual convention of the American Psychological Association, San Diego, CA.

Clanton Harpine, E. (2011a). *Group-centered prevention programs for at-risk students*. New York: Springer.

Clanton Harpine, E. (2011b, August). *Developing group-centered prevention programs for community-based settings*. Paper presented at the annual convention of the American Psychological Association, Washington, DC.

Clanton Harpine, E. (2012, August). *Prevention and change in low socioeconomic neighborhoods: Developing community programs that work—creative art interventions for change with children and teens*. Paper presented at the annual convention of the American Psychological Association, Orlando, FL.

Clanton Harpine, E. (2013a). *Erasing failure in the classroom, vol.3: The Reading Orienteering Club, using vowel clustering in an after-school program*. Aiken, SC: Group-Centered Learning.

Clanton Harpine, E. (2013b). *Prevention groups*. Thousand Oaks, CA: Sage.

Clanton Harpine, E., Nitza, A., & Conyne, R. (2010). Prevention groups: Today and tomorrow. *Group Dynamics: Theory, Research, and Practice, 14*, 268–280. doi:10.1037/a0020579.

Clanton Harpine, E., & Reid, T. (2009a). Enhancing academic achievement in a Hispanic immigrant community: The role of reading in academic failure and mental health. *School Mental Health, 1*, 159–170. doi:10.1007/s12310-009-9011-z.

Clanton Harpine, E., & Reid, T. (2009b, August). *The community's role in school prevention programs: Today and tomorrow*. Workshop presented at the annual convention of the American Psychological Association, Toronto, Canada.

Coie, J. D., Watt, N. F., West, S. G., Hawkins, J. D., Asarnow, J. R., Markham, H. J., et al. (1993). The science of prevention: A conceptual framework and some directions for a national research program. *American Psychologist, 48*, 1013–1022.

Condry, J., & Chambers, J. (1978). Intrinsic motivation and the process of learning. In M. R. Lepper & D. Greene (Eds.), *The hidden costs of reward: New perspectives on the psychology of human motivation*. Hillsdale, NJ: Lawrence Erlbaum.

Conyne, R. K. (2004). Prevention groups. In J. L. DeLucia-Waack, D. A. Gerrity, C. R. Kalodner, & M. T. Riva (Eds.), *Handbook of group counseling and psychotherapy* (pp. 621–629). Thousand Oaks, CA: Sage.

Conyne, R. K., & Clanton Harpine, E. (2010). Prevention groups: The shape of things to come. *Group Dynamics: Theory, Research, and Practice, 14*, 193–198. doi:10.1037/a0020446.

Cooper, H., Robinson, J. C., & Patall, E. A. (2006). Does homework improve academic achievement? A synthesis of research, 1987–2003. *Review of Educational Research, 76*(1), 1–62. doi:10.3102/003465430760010 01.

Cornelius, M. D., Goldschmidt, L., Day, N. L., & Larkby, C. (2002). Alcohol, tobacco and marijuana use among pregnant teenagers: 6-year follow-up of off-spring growth effects. *Neurotoxicology & Teratology, 24*, 703–710.

Criss, M. M., Pettit, G. S., Bates, J. E., Dodge, K. A., & Lapp, A. L. (2002). Family adversity, positive peer relationships, and children's externalizing behavior: A longitudinal perspective on risk and resilience. *Child Development, 73*, 1220–1237.

Deci, E. (1971). Effects of externally mediated rewards on intrinsic motivation. *Journal of Personality and Social Psychology, 18*, 105–115.

Deci, E. L. (2009). Large-scale school reform as viewed from self-determination theory perspective. *Theory in Education, 7*, 244–252.

Deci, E. L., Nezlek, J., & Sheinman, L. (1981). Characteristics of the rewarder and intrinsic motivation of the rewardee. *Journal of Personality and Social Psychology, 40*, 1–10.

Deci, E. L., & Ryan, R. M. (1985). *Intrinsic motivation and self-determination in human behavior.* New York: Plenum.

Deci, E. L., & Ryan, R. M. (2000). The Bwhat" and Bwhy" of goal pursuit: Human needs and the self-determination theory of behavior. *Psychology Inquiry, 11*, 227–268.

Deci, E. L., Ryan, R. M., & Williams, G. C. (1996). Need satisfaction and the self-regulation of learning. *Learning and Individual Differences, 8*, 165–183.

Deci, E., Vallerand, R., Pelletler, L., & Ryan, R. (1991). Motivation and education: The self-determination perspective. *Educational Psychologist, 26*, 325–347.

Draganski, B., Gaser, C., Kempermann, G., Kuhm, H. G., Winkler, J., Buchel, C., et al. (2006). Temporal and spatial dynamics of brain structure changes during extensive learning. *Journal of Neuroscience, 26*, 6314–6317.

Duckworth, A. L., Peterson, C., Matthews, M. D., & Kelly, D. R. (2007). Grit: Perseverance and passion for long-term goals. *Journal of Personality and Social Psychology, 92*, 1087–1101.

DuPaul, G. J., & Stoner, G. D. (2004). *ADHD in the schools: Assessment and intervention strategies* (2nd ed.). New York: Guilford Press.

DuPaul, G. J., & Weyandt, L. L. (2006). School-based intervention for children with Attention Deficit Hyperactivity Disorder: Effects on academic, social, and behavioural functioning. *International Journal of Disability, Development and Education, 53*, 161–176. doi:10.1080/10349120600716141.

Durlak, J. A., & Dupre, E. P. (2008). Implementation matters: A review of research on the influence of implementation on program outcomes and the factors affecting implementation. *American Journal of Community Psychology, 41*, 327–350.

Durlak, J. A., Mahoney, J. L., Bohnert, A. M., & Parente, M. E. (2010a). Developing and improving after-school programs to enhance youth's personal growth and adjustment: A special issue. *American Journal of Community Psychology, 45*, 285–293. doi:10.1007/s10464-010-9298-9.

Durlak, J. A., Weissberg, R. P., & Pachan, M. (2010b). A meta-analysis of after-school programs that seek to promote personal and social skills in children and adolescents. *American Journal of Community Psychology, 45*, 294–309. doi:10.1007/s10464-010-9300-6.

Ediger, M. (2002). Developing a reading community. *Journal of Instructional Psychology, 29*, 86–89.

Edwards, L. M., & Lopez, S. J. (2006). Perceived family support, acculturation, and life satisfaction in Mexican American youth: A mixed-methods exploration. *Journal of Counseling Psychology, 53*, 279–287.

Fall, M. (1999). A play therapy intervention and its relationship to self-efficacy and learning behaviors. *Professional School Counseling, 2*, 194–205.

Fall, M., & McLeod, E. H. (2001). Identifying and assisting children with low self-efficacy. *Professional School Counseling, 4*, 334–342.

Fawson, P. C., & Moore, S. A. (1999). Reading incentive programs: Beliefs and practices. *Reading Psychology, 20*, 325–340.

Finn, J. D., Gerber, S. B., & Boyd-Zaharias, J. (2005). Small classes in the early grades, academic achievement, and graduating from high school. *Journal of Educational Psychology, 97*, 214–223.

Fleming, C. B., Harachi, T. W., Cortes, R. C., Abbott, R. D., & Catalano, R. F. (2004). Level and change in reading scores and attention problems during elementary school as predictors of problem behavior in middle school. *Journal of Emotional and Behavioral Disorders, 12*, 130–144.

Foorman, B. R., Breier, J. I., & Fletcher, J. M. (2003). Interventions aimed at improving reading success: An evidence-based approach. *Developmental Neuropsychology, 24*, 613–639.

Fredricks, J. A., & Eccles, J. S. (2006). Is extracurricular participation associated with beneficial outcomes? Concurrent and longitudinal relations. *Development Psychology, 42*, 698–713.

Fuhriman, A., & Burlingame, G. M. (1994). Group psychotherapy: Research and practice. In A. Fuhriman & G. M. Burlingame (Eds.), *Handbook of group psychotherapy: An empirical and clinical synthesis* (pp. 3–40). New York: Wiley.

Gazda, G. M., Ginter, E. J., & Horne, A. M. (2001). *Group counseling and group psychotherapy: Theory and application.* Boston: Allyn & Bacon.

Gershoff, E. T. (2010). More harm than good: A summary of scientific research on the intended and unintended effects of corporal punishment on children. *Law and Contemporary Problems, 73*, 31–56.

Gersten, R., & Baker, S. (2001). Teaching expressive writing to students with learning disabilities: A meta-analysis. *Elementary School Journal, 97*, 475–500.

Gloria, A. M., Castellanos, J., & Orozco, V. (2005). Perceived educational barriers, cultural fit, coping responses, and psychological well-being of Latina undergraduates. *Hispanic Journal of Behavioral Sciences, 27*, 161–183.

Goldschmidt, L., Richardson, G. A., Cornelius, M. D., & Day, N. L. (2004). Prenatal marijuana and alcohol exposure and academic achievement at age 10. *Neurotoxicology & Teratology, 26*, 521–532.

Goldschmidt, L., Richardson, G. A., Willford, J., & Day, N. L. (2008). Prenatal marijuana exposure and intelligence test performance at age 6. *Journal of the American Academy of Child and Adolescent Psychiatry, 47*, 254–263.

Goldston, D. B., Davis Molock, S., Whitbeck, L. B., Murakami, J. L., Zayas, L. H., & Nagayama Hall, G. C. (2008). Cultural considerations in adolescent suicide prevention and psychosocial treatment. *American Psychologist, 63*, 14–31.

Gottfredson, D. C., Gerstenblith, S. A., Soule, D. A., Womer, S. C., & Lu, S. (2004). Do ASP's reduce delinquency? *Prevention Science, 5*, 253–266.

Graham, S., & Harris, K. R. (2003). Students with learning disabilities and the process of writing: A meta-analysis of SRSD studies. In H. L. Swanson, K. R. Harris, & S. Graham (Eds.), *Handbook of learning disabilities* (pp. 323–344). New York: Guilford Press.

Granger, R. C. (2010). Understanding and improving the effectiveness of after-school practice. *American Journal of Community Psychology, 45*, 441–446. doi:10.1007/s10464-010-9301-5.

Granger, R. C., Durlak, J., Yohalem, N., & Reisner, E. (2007). *Improving after-school program quality.* New York: William T. Grant Foundation.

Greenberg, M., Domitrovich, C., & Bumbarger, B. (2001). The prevention of mental disorders in school-aged children: Current state of the field. *Prevention and Treatment, 4*, Article 0001a. Retrieved May 9, 2005, from http://journals.apa.org/prevention/volume 4/pre0040001a.html.

Greenberg, M., Weissberg, R. P., O'Brien, M. U., Zins, J. E., Fredricks, L., Resnick, H., et al. (2003). Enhancing school-based prevention and youth development through coordinated social, emotional, and academic learning. *American Psychologist, 58*, 466–474. doi:10.1037/0003-066X.58.6-7.466.

Greene, J. P., & Winters, M. (2006). *Leaving boys behind: Public high school graduation rates.* New York: Manhattan Institute for Policy Research.

Gromoske, A. N., & Maguire-Jack, K. (2012). Transactional and cascading relations between early spanking and children's social-emotional development. *Journal of Marriage and Family, 74*, 1054–1068. doi:10.1111/j.1741-3737.2012.01013x.

Gullotta, T. P., Bloom, M., Gullotta, C., & Messina, J. C. (2009). *A blueprint for promoting academic and social competence in afterschool programs.* New York: Springer.

Hawkins, J. D., Catalano, R. F., Kosterman, R., Abbott, R., & Hill, K. G. (1999). Preventing adolescent health-risk behaviors by strengthening protection during childhood. *Archives of Pediatrics and Adolescent Medicine, 153,* 226–234.

Herman, K. C., Lambert, S. F., Reinke, W. M., & Ialongo, N. S. (2008). Low academic competence in first grade as a risk factor for depressive cognitions and symptoms in middle school. *Journal of Counseling Psychology, 55,* 400–410.

Herman, K. C., & Ostrander, R. O. (2007). The effects of attention problems on depression: Developmental, cognitive, and academic pathways. *School Psychology Quarterly, 22,* 483–510.

Hill, S. (Ed.). (2008). *Afterschool matters: Creative programs that connect youth development and student achievement.* Thousand Oaks, CA: Corwin Press.

Hirsch, J., Mekinda, M. A., & Stawicki, J. (2010). More than attendance: The importance of afterschool program quality. *American Journal of Community Psychology, 45,* 447–452. doi:10.1007/s10464-010-9310-4.

Hoag, M. J., & Burlingame, G. M. (1997). Evaluating the effectiveness of child and adolescent group treatment: A meta-analytic review. *Journal of Clinical Child Psychology, 26,* 234–246.

Hogg, M. A., Abrams, D., Otten, S., & Hinkle, S. (2004). The social identity perspective: Intergroup relations, self-conception, and small groups. *Small Group Research, 35,* 246–276.

Hoglund, W. L., & Leadbeater, B. J. (2004). The effects of family, school, and classroom ecologies on changes in children's social competence and emotional and behavioral problems in first grade. *Developmental Psychology, 40,* 533–544.

Holmes, S. E., & Kivlighan, D. M. (2000). Comparison of therapeutic factors in group and individual treatment processes. *Journal of Counseling Psychology, 47,* 478–484.

Holtz, R. (2004). Group cohesion, attitude projection, and opinion certainty: Beyond interaction. *Group Dynamics: Theory, Research, and Practice, 8,* 112–125.

Horne, A. M., Stoddard, J. L., & Bell, C. D. (2007). Group approaches to reducing aggression and bullying in school. *Group Dynamics: Theory, Research, and Practice, 11,* 262–271. doi:10.1037/1089-2699.11.4.262.

Huang, L., Stroul, B., Friedman, R., Mrazek, P., Friesen, B., Pires, S., et al. (2005). Transforming mental health care for children and their families. *American Psychologist, 60,* 615–627.

Invernizzi, M., Rosemary, C., Juel, C., & Richards, H. (1997). At-risk readers and community volunteers: A three-year perspective. *Journal of Scientific Studies in Reading, 1,* 277–300.

Jensen, P. S., Arnold, L. E., Swanson, J. M., Vitiello, B., Abikoff, H. B., Greenhill, L. L., et al. (2007). 3-year follow-up of the NIMH MTA study. *Journal of the American Academy of Child and Adolescent Psychiatry, 46,* 989–1002. doi:10.1097/CHI.0b013e3180886d48.

Katz, I., & Assor, A. (2007). When choice motivates and when it does not. *Educational Psychological Review, 19,* 429–442.

Kaye, C. B. (2004). *The complete guide to service learning: Proven, practical ways to engage students in civic responsibility, academic curriculum, & social action.* Minneapolis, Minn.: Free Spirit Publishing.

Kazak, A. E., Hoagwood, K., Weisz, J. R., Hood, K., Kratochwill, T. R., Vargas, L. A., et al. (2010). A meta-systems approach to evidence-based practice for children and adolescents. *American Psychologist, 65,* 85–97. doi:10.1037/a0017784.

Kazdin, A. E. (2008). Evidence-based treatment and practice: New opportunities to bridge clinical research and practice, enhance the knowledge base, and improve patient care. *American Psychologist, 63,* 146–159. doi:10.1037/0003-066X.63.3.146.

Kellam, S. G., Rebok, G. W., Mayer, L. S., Ialongo, N., & Kalodner, C. R. (1994). Depressive symptoms over first grade and their response to a developmental epidemiological based preventive trial aimed at improving achievement. *Development and Psychopathology, 6,* 463–481.

Keller, T. A., & Just, M. A. (2009). Altering cortical connectivity: Remediation-induced changes in the white matter of poor readers. *Neuron, 64,* 624–631. doi:10.1016/j.neuron.2009.10.018.

Klingberg, T., Forssberg, H., & Westerberg, H. (2002). Training of working memory in children with ADHD. *Journal of Clinical and Experimental Neuropsychology, 24*, 781–791.

Koegel, L. K., Kuriakose, S., Singh, A. K., & Koegel, R. L. (2012). Improving generalization of peer socialization gains in inclusive school settings using initiatives training. *Behavior Modification, 20*(10), 1–17. doi:10.1177/0145445512445609.

Kulic, K. R., Horne, A. M., & Dagley, J. C. (2004). A comprehensive review of prevention groups for children and adolescents. *Group Dynamics: Theory, Research, and Practice, 8*, 139–151.

Langley, A. K., Nadeem, E., Kataoka, S. H., Stein, B. D., & Jaycox, L. H. (2010). Evidence-based mental health programs in schools: Barriers and facilitators of successful implementation. *School Mental Health, 2*, 105–113. doi:10.1007/s12310-010-9038-1.

Larsen, R. J., & Ketelaar, T. (1991). Personality and susceptibility to positive and negative emotional states. *Journal of Personality and Social Psychology, 61*, 132–140.

Laska, K. M., Smith, T. L., Wislocki, A. P., Minami, T., & Wampold, B. E. (2013). Uniformity of evidence-based treatments in practice? Therapist effects in the delivery of cognitive processing therapy for PTSD. *Journal of Counseling Psychology, 60*, 31–41. doi:10.1037/a0031294.

Lauer, P. A., Akiba, M., Wilkerson, S. B., Apthorp, H. S., Snow, D., & Martin-Green, M. (2006). Out-of-school time programs: A meta-analysis of effects on at-risk students. *Review of Educational Research, 76*, 275–313.

Lepper, M. R., & Greene, D. (1975). Turning play into work: Effects of adult surveillance and extrinsic rewards on children's intrinsic motivation. *Journal of Personality and Social Psychology, 31*, 479–486.

Levin, H., & Holmes, N. (2005). American's learning deficit. *New York Times*, p. A25.

Lewis, B. A., Singer, L. T., Short, E., Minnes, S., Arendt, R., Weishampel, P., et al. (2004). Four-year language outcomes of children exposed to cocaine in utero. *Neurotoxicology & Teratology, 26*, 617–628.

Linnenbrink, E. A., & Pintrich, P. R. (2002). Motivation as an enabler for academic success. *School Psychology Review, 31*, 313–327.

Lugo Steidel, A., & Contreras, J. (2003). A new Familism Scale for use with Latino populations. *Hispanic Journal of Behavioral Sciences, 25*, 312–330.

Lusebrink, V. B. (2010). Assessment and therapeutic application of the expressive therapies continuum. *Art Therapy: Journal of the American Art Therapy Association, 24*, 166–170.

Lyon, G. R. (1998, April 28). *Overview of reading and literacy initiatives.* Testimony before the Committee on Labor and Human Resources, Senate Dirkson Building. Retrieved November 27, 2006, from http://www.cdl.org/resourcelibrary/pdf/lyon_testimonies.pdf

Lyon, G. R. (2002). Reading development, reading difficulties, and reading instruction educational and public health issues. *Journal of School Psychology, 40*, 3–6.

Mahoney, J. L., & Stattin, H. (2000). Leisure activities and adolescent antisocial behavior: The role of structure and social context. *Journal of Adolescence, 23*, 113–127.

Malchiodi, C. A. (2007). *The art therapy sourcebook.* New York: McGraw Hill.

Malchiodi, C. A. (Ed.). (2011). *Handbook of art therapy.* New York: Guilford Press.

Marmarosh, C., Holtz, A., & Schottenbauer, M. (2005). Group cohesiveness, group-derived collective self-esteem, group-derived hope, and the well-being of group therapy members. *Group Dynamics: Theory Research and Practice, 9*, 32–44.

Maugban, R. R., Rowe, R., Loeber, R., & Stouthamer-Loeber, M. (2003). Reading problems and depressed mood. *Journal of Abnormal Child Psychology, 31*, 219–229.

McCall, R. B., & Green, B. L. (2004). Beyond the methodological gold standards of behavioral research: Considerations for practice and policy. *Social Policy Report, 18*(3–4), 6–12.

McHugh, R. K., & Barlow, D. H. (2010). The dissemination and implementation of evidence-based psychological treatments: A review of current efforts. *American Psychologist, 65*, 73–84. doi:10.1037/a0018121.

McWhirter, J. J., McWhirter, B. T., McWhirter, E. H., & McWhirter, R. J. (2007). *At risk youth: A comprehensive response for counselors, teachers, psychologists, and human services professionals* (4th ed.). Belmont, CA: Thomson Brooks/Cole.

Merzenich, M. M. (2001). Cortical plasticity contributing to child development. In J. L. McClelland & R. S. Siegler (Eds.), *Mechanisms of cognitive development: Behavioral and neural perspectives* (pp. 67–95). Mahwah, NJ: Erlbaum.

Meyler, A., Keller, T. A., Cherkassky, V. L., Gabrieli, J. D., & Just, M. A. (2008). Modifying the brain activation of poor readers during sentence comprehension with extended remedial instruction: A longitudinal study of neuroplasticity. *Neuropsychologia, 46*, 2580–2592.

Miech, R. A., Eaton, W. W., & Brennan, K. (2005). Mental health disparities across education and sex: A prospective analysis examining how they persist over the life course. *Journals of Gerontology, 60B*, 93–98.

Miller, R. L., & Shinn, M. (2005). Learning from communities: Overcoming difficulties in the dissemination of prevention and promotion efforts. *American Journal of Community Psychology, 35*, 169–183.

Moradi, B., & Risco, C. (2006). Perceived discrimination experiences and mental health of Latina/o American persons. *Journal of Counseling Psychology, 53*, 411–421.

Morgan, P. L., Furkas, G., Tufis, P. A., & Sperling, R. A. (2008). Are reading and behavior problems risk factor for each other? *Journal of Learning Disabilities, 41*, 417–436. doi:10.1177/0022219408321123.

Morgan, A. E., Hynd, G. W., Riccio, C. A., & Hall, J. (1996). Validity of *DSM–IV* ADHD predominantly inattentive and combined types: Relationship to previous *DSM* diagnoses/subtype differences. *Journal of the American Academy of Child and Adolescent Psychiatry, 35*, 325–333.

Morris, D. (1999). *The Howard Street tutoring manual: Teaching at-risk readers in the primary grades*. New York: Guilford Press.

Nastasi, B. K., Moore, R. B., & Varjas, K. M. (2004). *School-based mental health services: Creating comprehensive and culturally specific programs*. Washington, DC: American Psychological Association.

Nation, M., Crusto, C., Wandersman, A., Kumpfer, K. L., Seybolt, D., Morrissey-Kane, E., et al. (2003). What works in prevention: Principles of effective prevention programs. *American Psychologist, 58*, 449–456. doi:10.1037/0003-066X.58.6-7.449.

National Assessment of Educational Progress. (2009). *Nation's Report Card: Reading 2009*. Retrieved from http://nces.ed.gov/nations report card/pdf/main2009/2010458.pdf.

National Center for Education Statistics. (2011). *The Nation's Report Card: Reading 2011* (NCES 2012–457). National Center for educational statistics, Institute of education sciences, US Department of Education, Washington DC.

National Household Education Survey. Retrieved February 2, 2007, from The National Center for Education Statistics … National Household Education Survey … National Center for Education Statistics- http://nces.ed.gov

National Reading Panel. (2000). *Teaching children to read: An evidence-based assessment of the scientific research literature on reading and its implications for reading instruction (NIH Publication No. 00–4754)*. Washington, DC: National Institute for Literacy.

Nelson, C. A., & Bosquet, M. (2000). Neurobiology of fetal and infant development: Implications for infant mental health. In C. H. Zeanah Jr. (Ed.), *Handbook of infant mental health* (2nd ed.). New York: Guilford Press.

Nelson, G., Westhues, A., & MacLeod, J. (2003). A meta-analysis of longitudinal research on preschool prevention programs for children. *Prevention and Treatment, 6*, Article 0031a. Retrieved May 9, 2005, from http://journals.apa.org/prevention/volume 6/preoo60031a.html.

Nikulina, V., Widom, C. S., & Czaja, S. (2011). The role of childhood neglect and childhood poverty in predicting mental health, academic achievement and crime in adulthood. *American Journal of Community Psychology, 48*, 309–321. doi:10.1007/s10464-010-9385-y.

Noam, G. C., & Hermann, C. A. (2002). Where education and mental health meet: Developmental prevention and early intervention in schools. *Developmental Psychopathology, 14*, 861–875.

Obiakor, F. E. (2001). *It even happens in "good" schools: Responding to cultural diversity in today's classrooms*. Thousand Oaks, CA: Sage.

Ogrodniczuk, J. S., & Piper, W. E. (2003). The effect of group climate on outcome in two forms of short-term group therapy. *Group Dynamics: Theory Research and Practice, 7*, 64–76.

Orfield, G., & Lee, C. (2005). *Why segregation matters: Poverty and educational inequality.* Cambridge, MA: The Civil Right Project at Harvard University.

Ozsivadjian, A., & Knott, F. (2011). Anxiety problems in young people with autism spectrum disorder: A case series. *Clinical Child Psychology and Psychiatry, 16*, 203–214. doi:10.117711359104511404 749.

Pierce, K. M., Bolt, D. M., & Vandell, D. L. (2010). Specific features of after-school program quality: associations with children's functioning in middle childhood. *American Journal of Community Psychology, 45*, 381–393. doi:10.1007/s10464-010-9304-2.

Pintrich, P. R., & Schunk, D. H. (2002). *Motivation in education: Theory, research, and applications* (2nd ed.). New Jersey: Prentice Hall.

Posthuma, B. W. (2002). *Small groups in counseling and therapy: Process and leadership* (4th ed.). Boston, MA: Allyn and Bacon.

Pressley, M., Mohan, L., Raphael, L. M., & Fingeret, L. (2007). How does Bennett Woods Elementary School produce such high reading and writing achievement? *Journal of Educational Psychology, 99*, 221–240.

Prilleltensky, I., Nelson, G., & Pierson, L. (2001). The role of power and control in children's lives: An ecological analysis of pathways toward wellness, resilience and problems. *Journal of Community and Applied Social Psychology, 11*, 143–158.

Rayner, K., Foorman, B. R., Perfetti, C. A., Pesetsky, D., & Seidenberg, M. S. (2001). How psychological science informs the teaching of reading. *Psychological Science in the Public Interest, 2*, 31–74. doi:10.1111/1529-10006.00004.

Reeve, J., Nix, G., & Hamm, D. (2003). The experience of self-determination in intrinsic motivation and the conundrum of choice. *Journal of Educational Psychology, 95*, 347–392.

Reeve, J., Ryan, R. M., Deci, E. L., & Jang, H. (2007). Understanding and promoting autonomous self-regulation: A self-determination theory perspective. In D. Schunk & B. Zimmerman (Eds.), *Motivation and self-regulated learning: Theory, research, practice* (pp. 223–244). Mahwah, NJ: Lawrence Erlbaum Associates Publishing.

Riggs, N. R., Bohnert, A. M., Guzman, M. D., & Davidson, D. (2010). Examining the potential of community-based after-school programs for latino youth. *American Journal of Community Psychology, 45*, 417–429. doi:10.1007/s10464-010-9313-1.

Riggs, N. R., & Greenberg, M. T. (2004). After-school youth development programs can be effective for solving academic failure and reducing crime. *Clinical Child and Family Psychology Review, 7*, 177–190.

Rodriguez, N., Bingham Mira, C., Paez, N. D., & Myers, H. F. (2007). Exploring the complexities of familism and acculturation: Central constructs for People of Mexican origin. *American Journal of Community Psychology, 39*, 61–77.

Rogers, C. (1969). *Freedom to learn.* Columbus, OH: Merrill.

Romero, A. J., & Roberts, R. E. (2003). Stress within a bicultural context for adolescents of Mexican descent. *Cultural Diversity and Ethnic Minority Psychology, 9*, 171–184.

Roth, J. L., Malone, L. M., & Brooks-Gunn, J. (2010). Does the amount of participation in after-school programs relate to developmental outcomes? A review of the literature. *American Journal of Community Psychology, 45*, 310–324. doi:10.1007/s10464-010-9303-3.

Rubin, J. A. (2005). *Child art therapy: 25th anniversary edition.* Hoboken, NJ: John Wiley.

Ryan, R. M., & Deci, E. L. (2000). Intrinsic and extrinsic motivations: Classic definitions and new directions. *Contemporary Educational Psychology, 25*, 54–67.

Ryan, R. M., & Deci, E. L. (2008). Self-determination theory and the role of basic psychological needs and personality and the organization of behavior. In O. P. John, R. W. Robbins, & L. A. Pervin (Eds.), *Handbook of personality: Theory and research* (pp. 654–678). New York: The Guilford Press.

Sale, E., Sambrano, S., Springer, J. F., Peña, C., Pan, W., & Kasim, R. (2005). Family protection and prevention of alcohol use among Hispanic youth at high risk. *American Journal of Community Psychology, 36*, 195–205.

Salovey, P., Rothman, A. J., Detweiler, J. B., & Steward, W. T. (2000). Emotional states physical health. *American Psychologist, 55*, 110–121.

Sandler, I., Ostrom, A., Bitner, M. J., Ayers, T. S., Wolchik, S., & Daniels, V. S. (2005). Developing effective prevention services for the real world: A prevention service development model. *American Journal of Community Psychology, 35*, 127–142.

Segal, N. L. (2000). *Entwined lives: Twins and what they tell us about human behavior*. New York: Plume.

Seligman, M. E. P. (1990). *Learned optimism: How to change your mind and your life*. New York: Pocket Books.

Sheldon, J., Arbreton, A., Hopkins, L., & Grossman, J. B. (2010). Investing in success: Key strategies for building quality in after-school programs. *American Journal of Community Psychology, 45*, 394–404. doi:10.1007/s10464-010-9296-y.

Shernoff, D. J. (2010). Engagement in after-school programs as a predictor of social competence and academic performance. *American Journal of Community Psychology, 45*, 325–337. doi:10.1007/s10464-010-9314-0.

Simonsen, B., Shaw, S. F., Sugai, G., Coyne, M. D., Rhein, B., Madaus, J. W., et al. (2010). A schoolwide model for service delivery: Redefining special educators as interventionists. *Remedial and Special Education, 31*(1), 17–23. doi:10.1177/0741932508324396.

Slavin, R. L. (2002). Operative group dynamics in school settings: Structuring to enhance educational, social, and emotional progress. *Group, 26*, 297–308.

Slavin, R. E., & Madden, N. A. (2001). *Success for all: Research and reform in elementary education*. Mahwah, NY: Lawrence Erlbaum.

Smith, C., Peck, S. C., Denault, A.-S., Blazevski, J., & Akiva, T. (2010). Quality at the point of service: Profiles of practice in after-school settings. *American Journal of Community Psychology, 45*, 358–369. doi:10.1007/s10464-010-9315-z.

Snowden, L. R. (2005). Racial, cultural and ethnic disparities in health and mental health: Toward theory and research at community levels. *American Journal of Community Psychology, 35*, 1–8.

Sternberg, R. J. (2005). Intelligence, competence, and expertise. In A. J. Elliot & C. S. Dweck (Eds.), *Handbook of competence and motivation* (pp. 15–30). New York: The Guilford Press.

Sternberg, R. J., Wagner, R. K., Williams, W. M., & Horvath, J. A. (1997). Testing common sense. In D. Russ-Eft, H. Preskill, & C. Sleezer (Eds.), *Human resource development review: Research and implications* (pp. 102–132). Thousand Oaks, CA: Sage.

Stone, D., Deci, E. L., & Ryan, R. M. (2009). Beyond talk: Creating autonomous motivation through self-determination theory. *Journal of General Management, 34*, 75–91.

Strayhorn, J. (2002). Self-control: Toward systematic training programs. *Journal of the American Academy of Child and Adolescent Psychiatry, 41*, 17–27.

Suarez-Orozco, C., & Suarez-Orozco, M. M. (2001). *Children of immigration*. Cambridge, MA: Harvard University Press.

Thorkildsen, T. A. (2002). Literacy as a lifestyle: Negotiating the curriculum to facilitate motivation. *Reading and Writing Quarterly, 18*, 321–328.

Toppelberg, C. O., Munir, K., & Nieto-Castañon, A. (2006). Spanish-English bilingual children with psychopathology: Language deficits and academic language proficiency. *Child and Adolescent Mental Health, 11*, 156–163.

Torgesen, J. K., Alexander, A. W., Wagner, R. K., Rashotte, C. A., Voeller, K. S., & Conway, T. (2001). Intensive remedial instruction for children with severe reading disabilities: Immediate and long-term outcomes from two instructional approaches. *Journal of Learning disabilities, 34*, 133–158. doi:10.1177/002221940103400104.

Trout, A. L., Lienemann, T. O., Reid, R., & Epstein, M. H. (2007). A review of non-medication interventions to improve the academic performance of children and youth with ADHD. *Remedial and Special Education, 28*, 207–226.

Twenge, J., & Campbell, W. K. (2002). Self-esteem and socioeconomic status: A meta-analytic review. *Personality and Social Psychology Review, 6*, 59–71.

U. S. Department of Education. (2009). *21st Century community learning centers*. Retrieved July 12, 2010, from http://www.ed.gov/programs/21stcclc/index.html

U. S. Public Health Service. (2000). *Report of the Surgeon General's Conference on Children's Mental Health: A national action agenda*. Washington, DC: U. S. Department of health and Human Services. Retrieved from http://www.gurgeongeneral.gov/library/mentalhealth/chapter3/sec.1.html

Urdan, T., & Turner, J. C. (2005). Competence motivation in the classroom. In A. J. Elliot & C. S. Dweck (Eds.), *Handbook of competence and motivation* (pp. 297–317). New York: The Guilford Press.

Vacha-Haase, T., & Thompson, B. (2004). How to estimate and interpret effect sizes. *Journal of Counseling Psychology, 51*, 473–481.

Vansteenkiste, M., & Deci, E. L. (2003). Competitively contingent rewards and intrinsic motivation: Can losers remain motivated? *Motivation and Emotion, 27*, 273–299.

Wandersman, A., Duffy, J., Flaspohler, P., Norman, R., Lubell, K., Stillman, L., et al. (2008). Bridging the gap between prevention research and practice: The interactive systems framework for dissemination and implementation. *American Journal of Community Psychology, 41*, 171–181. doi:10.1007/s10464-008-9174-z.

Wandersman, A., & Florin, P. (2003). Community interventions and effective prevention. *American Psychologist, 58*, 441–448. doi:10.1037/0003-066X.58.6-7.441.

Ward, S., Sylva, J., & Gresham, F. M. (2010). School-based predictors of early adolescent depression. *School Mental Health, 2*, 125–131. doi:10.1007/s12310-010-9028-3.

Weissberg, R., Kumpfer, K., & Seligman, M. (2003). Prevention that works for children and youth: An introduction. *American Psychologist, 58*, 425–432. doi:10.1037/0003-066X.58.6-7.425.

Yalom, I. D., & Leszcz, M. (2005). *The theory and practice of group psychotherapy* (5th ed.). New York: Basic Books.

Yohalem, N., & Wilson-Ahlstrom, A. (2010). Inside the black box: Assessing and improving quality in youth programs. *American Journal of Community Psychology, 45*, 350–357. doi:10.1007/s10464-010-9311-3.

Zayas, L., Lester, R., Cabassa, L., & Fortuna, L. (2005). "Why do so many Latina teens attempt suicide?" A conceptual model for research. *American Journal of Orthopsychiatry, 75*, 275–287.

Zea, M. C., Asner-Self, K. K., Birman, D., & Buki, L. P. (2003). The abbreviated multidimensional acculturation scale: Empirical validation with two Latino/Latina samples. *Cultural Diversity and Ethnic Minority Psychology, 9*, 107–126.

Zimmerman, B. J., Bonner, S., & Kovach, R. (1996). *Developing self-regulated learners: Beyond achievement to self-efficacy*. Washington, DC: American Psychological Association.

Zimmerman, B. J., & Kitsantas, A. (2005). The hidden dimension of personal competence: Self-regulated learning and practice. In A. J. Elliot & C. S. Dweck (Eds.), *Handbook of competence and motivation* (pp. 509–526). New York: The Guilford Press.

About the Author

Elaine Clanton Harpine, Ph.D., is a motivational psychologist specializing in group-centered motivational program design. She has 41 years of experience designing and conducting motivational prevention programs for children and youth. Dr. Clanton Harpine earned her doctorate in Educational Psychology, Counseling from the University of Illinois, Urbana-Champaign.

Dr. Clanton Harpine has published 14 nonfiction books, including *Prevention Groups* (2013), *Group-Centered Prevention Programs for At-Risk Students* (2011), *Group Interventions in Schools: Promoting Mental Health for At-Risk Children and Youth* (2008), and *No Experience Necessary!* which received an *Award of Excellence* in 1995 and was selected as one of the top five children's books in its class. Other published children's writings include a two-volume series entitled, *Come Follow Me*, in 2001; a three-volume family series completed in 2003; a youth book in 1989 along with numerous articles for teenagers on peer pressure, coping with failure, alcohol abuse, parents, suicide, and more recently, articles on using group-centered interventions in the schools. Other published writings include a series on *Erasing Failure in the Classroom,* a series of ready-to-use group-centered program packets: Vol. 1, *The Camp Sharigan Program* (*2nd ed.*, 2010), Vol. 2, *Vowel Clustering* (2010), and Vol. 3, the *Reading Orienteering Club* (2013).

Dr. Clanton Harpine has been interviewed on local early morning TV and radio concerning her workshop "Communication for Married Couples" and has been interviewed on local university radio concerning her work with inner-city children.

Her research for the past 12 years has focused on using group-centered interventions with at-risk readers. Dr. Clanton Harpine designed the motivational reading program called, *Camp Sharigan,* which she has used extensively in her work and research. She also designed the *Reading Orienteering Club* after-school prevention program and *4-Step Method* for teaching at-risk children to read. Her research with these programs has been published in psychological journals and reported through presentations at the American Psychological Association's annual conventions.

E. Clanton Harpine, *After-School Prevention Programs for At-Risk Students: Promoting Engagement and Academic Success*, DOI 10.1007/978-1-4614-7416-6, © Springer Science+Business Media New York 2013

In recent years, Dr. Clanton Harpine has been teaching Group Therapy and Counseling, Lifespan Development, and Human Growth and Development at the University of South Carolina Aiken and is continuing her research with group-centered prevention. She is the editor for the "Prevention Corner" column which appears quarterly in *The Group Psychologist*. She was selected for inclusion in *Who's Who of American Women*, 2006–2013 for her work with children in inner-city neighborhoods and at-risk communities.

Index

E. Clanton Harpine, *After-School Prevention Programs for At-Risk Students:*
Promoting Engagement and Academic Success, DOI 10.1007/978-1-4614-7416-6,
© Springer Science+Business Media New York 2013

CPSIA information can be obtained at www.ICGtesting.com
Printed in the USA
LVOW01*1701070114

368462LV00009B/287/P